What Others are Saying...

Making space to hear, to know, and to care for people "not in our tribe" may be one of the most urgent and transformative things we could be doing. In this bitterly divided era in American society and politics, may we who seek to be Jesus-followers live out our vocation as reconcilers and peacemakers with love and justice. *A Language of Healing* could be just the right practical help for our next steps at this important time.

MARK LABBERTON, President, Fuller Theological Seminary

A Language of Healing for a Polarized Nation is the book we need at this critical moment in our history. At a time when many Americans are reduced to shouting past one another, the authors of this volume—three thoughtful, compassionate citizens—give us a roadmap to restore civility and respect across even our deepest differences. Filled with honest dialogue, inspiring stories, and practical advice, this compelling volume should be required reading for every American committed to seeking a common vision for the common good.

DR. CHARLES C. HAYNES, Founding Director,
Religious Freedom Center of the Freedom Forum Institute

The conversation taking place in *A Language of Healing for a Polarized Nation* is one that needs to take place in coffee shops, board rooms, and living rooms, around fire pits and water coolers, and in the office—especially if it's an oval one. This book is a roadmap to compassion, understanding, and empathy at a time in which we seem to have lost the directions.

ERNIE JOHNSON, JR., Sportscaster, TNT/TBS, Author of *Unscripted: The Unpredictable Moments That Make Life Extraordinary*

A Language of Healing offers a path to communicating beyond deep differences. In today's world, even the slightest disagreements lead to hostility rather than a search for true common ground. This book offers solutions to coming away from divisiveness and shifting to generosity and respect. It is a must-read for anyone looking to flip the script.

SHANNON GROVE, California State Senate Republican Leader

In *A Language of Healing,* authors Wayne Jacobsen, Arnita Taylor, and Bob Prater absorb the reader in compelling conversations around challenging topics often held as unapproachable in polite company: namely race, politics, sexuality, and religion. People today find it increasingly difficult to hold civil conversations about such hot topics, especially with those of a different "tribe." The richness in this book is found in the authors divergence and consensus on finding "shared space" in the midst of tough topics and an increasingly uncivil society. While each writer brings differing backgrounds, experiences, and perspectives to the table, all seem to find a rich common ground surrounding the most divisive problems in our culture today. This is a must-read for anyone who cares about healing the rifts in our world today.

DR. JIM J. ADAMS, President Emeritus, Life Pacific University

Somehow, in each stage of a nation's life, a special book always seems to come along that is perfectly matched for its times. Most often such a book comes from a most unlikely source. At this deeply troubled time when our nation is tearing itself apart with hateful rancor, a wise and winsome source of help and healing has arisen out of a providential friendship between these three people. Bottom line: Our basic humanity will knit us all together in reasonable and workable harmony if we will dare to give friendship a chance.

DON CLARK, Former CBS News Anchor and current host of *Open Up Live*

A Language of Healing has arrived at a critical moment in a cultural landscape full of division. With intellect, humor, and compassion, this book invites you into a conversation between three unique thinkers, as they wrestle with issues that often divide. I genuinely found myself riveted to the point of screen-shooting my favorite pages. If you too, like me, long to grow in understanding cultural intelligence, compassion, and practical tools in navigating relationships at home, work, and in your community, you will be encouraged deeply by this work.

TRACY LEVINSON, Best-selling author of *Unashamed*

This dialogue takes us all in a much-needed direction. It guides us into an attempt to understand our differences and contemplate with more nuance the difficult issues we face. It helps us listen to each other; it boldly asks us to care for each other. It's a direction that catapults us from merely tolerating our differences to learning to appreciate them and respect our shared humanity.

EMAD J. MEERZA, Former Amir of the Muslims
of Bakersfield and Kern County

If ever a book was needed to help us understand the common ground of our humanity, it is now. Today, when so many long to practice peace but are at a loss to go about it, *A Language of Healing* provides hope, guidance, and inspiration. Communicating effectively requires finding—and then walking in—the shared space between us. In a world of runaway social media and chaotic twitter feed we need to find a way back to each other... back to our humanness. *A Language of Healing* resounds with a strong, collective voice that arises out of the diverse backgrounds and perspectives of the authors. As they model dialogue and work together to fashion a solution, motivation toward peace and reconciliation are sure to emerge in readers who are open to the transforming power of God through Christ. *A Language of Healing* is a gift from God! Thanks for this awesome book!

STEPHANIE BENNETT, PHD, Professor of Communication and
Media Ecology, Palm Beach Atlantic University and
author of the *Within the Walls* trilogy

A Language of Healing is a brave attempt to bring some sanity back into our national dialogue. You can be passionate for your views without diminishing those who think differently. Maybe if we actually listened to each other from hearts predisposed for compassion, we would find ways to work together for "a more perfect union." This insightful and compelling work offers the blueprints for a better conversation and a more gracious society.

JOHN LYNCH, Coauthor of *Bo's Cafe* and *The Cure* and author of *On My Worst Day*

Reading this book was like eavesdropping on an important conversation I needed to hear. It taught me a more nuanced way of speaking with people who don't look like me, vote like me, love like me, or worship like me. Evolving as a culture will require the generosity of many ordinary citizens who desire to learn this new language and are willing to risk being in close proximity to those different from themselves. This book gave me the courage to lean in and begin learning *A Language of Healing.*

ANNA LEBARON, Author of *The Polygamist's Daughter: A Memoir*

I hope for a more compassionate, thinking citizenry—more about us and less about we. This book will stimulate that dialogue as people learn to listen with compassion while recognizing personal bias. Encouraging understanding that "agreement isn't necessary, but respect is not optional," the authors recommend being "more human." In this toxic world of intolerance, this reader has hope for a new tomorrow with common ground for humanity to excel over "my way or the highway" behaviors among leaders.

MARTY BUTT BEERT, ED.D., Retired school superintendent,
Gig Harbor, WA

What a gift this is to so many! My friend Arnita Taylor truly lives the language of healing. I've watched her consistently and persistently extend kindness, welcome, and friendship to people of many different cultures and backgrounds in her straightforward and gracious way, even when met with resistance or rejection. I'm thrilled that she and her coauthors have offered such depth of insight and wisdom, helping us learn to approach all people with open minds, open hands, and open hearts. What a needed message.

CHERI COCHRAN, Director of Leadership Development,
Victory World Church, Atlanta, GA

In this contemptuous culture we are in desperate need of those who want to win the peace. *A Language of Healing* is not only easy to read but entertaining as well and offers us concrete steps to infuse the world with a new dialogue. Arnita, Bob, and Wayne lovingly equip and encourage us all to become catalysts for cultural change and to stand together to ensure justice and dignity for all humanity. Don't miss this book!

LEAH ANDREWS, Director, Siburt Institute at
Abilene Christian University

A Language of Healing is a book for everyone searching to understand and connect with their neighbor. It prepares its readers for difficult conversations and gives them permission to explore them. It is a book that helps us see the humanity in everyone and learn to communicate from that posture. The book asks us to show up fully—not shy away from who we are in our expressions of culture, gender, religion, and sexual orientation—and make room for others. This book is an important piece in a journey of healing and conciliation. It is a conduit that can lead us to lament with one another, to take up the cause of the marginalized, and to build communities that are truly equitable. Why not start with a conversation?

DIEULA PREVILION, Associate Pastor, Redeemer Covenant Church and
Founder and Executive Director, ElevateHer International

I am in awe of the ability of all three authors to stand in truth and speak in power to heal a nation. Their voices encourage us all to extend love to the "less loveable." A Language of Healing closes gaps while igniting the hard conversations that others often skirt.

ARLEANA WALLER, The ShePower Global Ambassador
Author of, *Host of the Pink Truth*

Our country certainly needs this important book. It is not only challenging and inspiring, it is also a metaphor for what our culture needs—people of different races, backgrounds, and political beliefs working together from our commonalities rather than our differences. The book asks, "What would happen if we all took custody of our culture?" We all need to answer this question and determine how we are contributing to today's divisive culture and assess our individual responsibility to bring healing to it.

PAUL SWEARENGIN, Author of *Joseph Comes to Town: When the Religious Right Goes Religiously Wrong* and host of *The Nonpartisan Evangelical*

In times of great division and animosity, *A Language of Healing* is not only a book that everyone should read, but a book that everyone must read. It is a well-articulated dialogue between three colleagues that explores the importance of valuing understanding, rather than agreement, and the importance of listening, rather than persuading. I would highly recommend that both the House and Senate have a mandatory book club with this as their first title! We need to be willing to create respect in difficult conversations, and *A Language of Healing* provides an excellent framework.

PASTRIX ANGIE GIA BENNETT, Magdalene Hope, Inc.

A Language of Healing is the spirit-child of Bob, Wayne, and Arnita but it has been my heart cry for the past 12 years. The honest, conversational style of this much-needed volume could be what helps to detonate the time bomb that seems to be ticking in our over-sensitized, and polarized discourse. I can't help but think that this book could be the antithesis of what was done at the Tower of Babel. Rather than confound the languages to stop us from moving forward, this work can serve to unite us around a common language that will heal the very ones who need it most.

GIL MICHEL, Lead Servant
That Church Downtown, South Bend, Indiana

Miss this book and you'll miss one of life's greatest joys—hearing the stories of people who view life differently than you do. I once was considered the most conservative Republican in the state Senate and was called upon to demonize the opposition. I finally figured out that as an unabashed follower of Jesus, my first responsibility is to make friends. And so, I have raised eyebrows among my conservative friends by inviting gay couples to dinner, befriending a Muslim student with no attempt to convert him, crying with a liberal Democrat colleague about a failed marriage, and inviting a Mormon bishop to talk at one of my Bible studies. Living out the ideas in this book has been one of the most satisfying journeys of my life. I hope you will do more than read the book—try to reach across to the other side.

TIM PHILPOT, Retired judge and author of *Judge Z: Irretrievably Broken*

At a time when politicians and media personalities maximize their exploitation of our baser instincts, it seems like more and more people, like myself, are refusing to blindly accept their poisonous potions. We're looking for ways to address real issues with real solutions. We refuse to sheepishly buy into mindless false binary choices. We refuse to demonize those who disagree with us. Now three brave souls have come to help us learn how to listen, how to get to know people unlike us, and how to build consensus in a way that nurtures community and advances healthy humanity. I pray this work reverses the tide of tiresome tribalism and helps to produce a critical mass of people who will pave a new path of hope and healing, instead of alienation and animosity.

VINCE COAKLEY, Host Vince Coakley Radio Program
1110 WBT, Charlotte, NC. and 106.3 WORD, Greenville, SC

A Language of Healing for a Polarized Nation

Creating safe environments for conversations about race, politics, sexuality, and religion

By
Wayne Jacobsen, Arnita Taylor,
and Bob Prater

International Standard Book Number
978-1-7340153-0-0

Copyright © 2019 by Wayne Jacobsen, Arnita Willis Taylor,
and Robert L. Prater

Blue Sheep Media
BlueSheepMedia.com
2902 East C Street | Torrington, WY 82240
p. 201.240.7106 | 213.408.9322
email: publish@bluesheepmedia.com

Cover and Interior designs: Charles Brock, www.brockbookdesignco.com

Printed in the United States of America
Original Printing November?

Dedication:

*To the God whose unwavering love
brought us together by the most absurd means possible
and allowed the three of us coauthors
to be included in a series of conversations
that were as delightful as they were transforming,
and to our families whose support and love
make our lives meaningful and made this book possible.*

CONTENTS

Section 1

An Opportune Moment

1. A Fork in the Road   25
2. What's in It for Me?   38
3. Pardon Me, Your Tribe Is Showing   49
4. The Symphony of Different   64
5. Staking Out the Common Ground   72

Section 2

Five Practices of a Peacemaker

6. Being Comfortable in Your Own Skin   89
7. Cultivating Compassion   100
8. Listen Up!   111
9. From My Good to Our Good   121
10. Willing to Be Disruptive   133

Section 3

Operating in Shared Space

11. Disarming the Binary Bomb   147
12. Bust Up Your Bias   158
13. Sharing the Table   170
14. Friendly Fire   180
15. Custodians of a Common Good   190

It doesn't matter if the group is a church or a

gang or a sewing circle or masculinity itself,

asking members to dislike, disown, or distance

themselves from another group of people as

a condition of 'belonging' is always about

control and power. I think we have to ques-

tion the intentions of any group that insists on

disdain toward other people as a membership

requirement."

— Brené Brown, in *Daring Greatly*

INTRODUCTION

Have you ever found yourself in an awkward moment with someone different from you? Maybe you both heard a joke at the same time, but your reactions were wildly different. Have you ever made a comment that you found out later was offensive to others, when you didn't mean it to be? Are you afraid to initiate a conversation with someone different from you for fear you'll say the wrong thing or be misinterpreted?

If you answered yes to any of these questions, you are in good company. Our social fabric is unraveling as anger and vitriol rule the national dialogue. Offenses are easily taken... and too often intended. We are losing our ability to communicate gracefully with people of different cultures, interest groups, or opinions.

Political parties exploit it, the media sells it, and Russian troll farms exacerbate it. And they will continue to as long as the electorate falls for it.

Aren't you done with all of that?

Our differences cannot be an excuse to vent our anger and animosity. We can hold to differing views and argue for them passionately without resorting to contempt, suspicion, and accusations. If we can manage this, we'll not only learn more about each other, but we might also find ways to work together for our shared interests, guarding our own dignity by giving it to others.

This is a book for those who are tired of being spun by politicians and media and having their personal relationships destroyed by differences in religion, race, sexuality, and politics. It's for those who want to find ways to communicate and cooperate beyond our most deeply rooted differences. It's for those who realize that in the shared spaces of our society we have more to gain through mutual understanding than from the politics of polarization.

If you enjoy the fight or profit by it in money, votes, or clicks, you will not enjoy this book. While it's not about linguistics per se, it is about speaking a language that dials down the anger and opens the door to listening to others as much as we want to be heard.

 The idea for this book began with Bob Prater, a former pastor, lumber company manager, entertainment developer, and father of three daughters. He spends a lot of his time with people who have been marginalized—the poor, the LGBTQ community, and others who've been abused or fallen through the cracks of our society. He's also been a bridge to the Muslim community in his own city of Bakersfield, California. His friendship with people in these groups, however, has caused great concern among his friends in the evangelical community.

 In 2017, he contacted his long-time friend, Wayne Jacobsen, asking him if he wanted to collaborate on a book about a language of healing. Wayne used to pastor in the religiously conservative area of Central California though he now lives in Southern California. He had spent the previous twenty-five years helping school districts and parent groups reach consensus agreements on a number of divisive issues, while simultaneously writing, publishing, and conducting seminars on spiritual intimacy around the world.

Bob thought their combined experiences could help dispel

the growing anger in our culture. In addition, Wayne is theologically and politically conservative, while Bob is more progressive on both scores. They have butted heads often on various issues, but through their conversations only grew closer as friends. Both disdain the polarizing rhetoric that has taken over the country.

Bob also had a third person in mind—a female politician in California who would bring more perspective to the conversation. Unfortunately, she bowed out in the end, and they began to seek another voice to enrich the content of the book. During that time, Wayne met with some people in a home in Dallas, Texas, when in walked Arnita Taylor, feigning frustration at having been passed over for the role of Papa in the movie *The Shack*, based on a book Wayne coauthored.

Arnita is an African-American woman from middle Tennessee, now living in a mostly white suburb. Arnita was trained as a laboratory chemist, raised two young men with her husband, earned a graduate degree in leadership development from Walden University, was employed in church ministry at a predominately white congregation, and is the founder of EIGHT Ministries (a consulting agency for leadership development).

During the meeting, comments were made displaying some insensitivity on racial issues. Before Wayne could jump in and help with any potential offense, Arnita spoke up. As Wayne recalled the conversation, in the most gracious way imaginable Arnita helped the room communicate more wisely and freely about racial differences. "Now, I'm not going to take offense to that," Arnita would say, "but this is how others I know might hear that..." Her honesty and demeanor invited others into a conversation and added to an already enriching discussion.

Wayne wondered at the time if she might be the third voice

they were looking for. Shortly after, Wayne called Bob and they discussed the possibility of adding Arnita to the authorship of *A Language of Healing*. After a few more meetings, it was clear that Arnita was the right fit for the project though they had no prior relationship with her.

Thus began *A Language of Healing...* During the course of writing together not only was Arnita a valuable contributor, but she also became a treasured friend. As you'll see, each chapter is written as a conversation between them, with sketches to help identify who is doing the talking in any given paragraph. Though framed as a conversation, the words were edited to flow seamlessly from paragraph to paragraph. However, in many cases, who was speaking was even more important than what was said to give the words context. You're invited to eavesdrop on their conversation and, by doing so, are encouraged to learn a different language for your own relationships.

None of them claim to be an expert in the language of healing, though they are avid learners. They are three very ordinary Americans, who are tired of the polarized rhetoric and name-calling that surround issues of religion, politics, sexuality and race. They all enjoy a number of deep friendships with people who have very different views and experiences, and they appreciate what they learn in those relationships. This is their appeal for all of us to seek better ways to communicate with our family and friends in these critical areas.

They are not social scientists using formal qualitative or quantitative research. They are concerned citizens, learning from one another while adding their own personal narratives. They are not writing for the politicians and pundits in Washington, D.C., but to other people who don't want differing perspectives to further divide us. They hope better dialogue and greater compassion will lead to more mutually satisfying answers to the problems we face.

None of them are trying to convince you their opinion is the right one, but rather they want to model how friends can talk through combustible issues. When you realize you don't have to convince people you are right and they are wrong, you get to grow by appreciating that others look at the world differently. The substance of their conversation is in their mutual respect and the desire to find a common ground larger than their own preferences.

Try it. You'll find that issues are more nuanced than you've been led to believe, and you may discover some rich friendships along the way.

The book is divided into three main sections:

- **An Opportune Moment.** Why is this a particularly propitious moment to elevate the conversation, at least for the vast majority of Americans who are tired of those who manipulate them through fear and anger?

- **Five Practices of a Peacemaker.** What does it take for someone to be in a conversation to help lower the heat and increase the level of communication, especially where we hold significantly different views?

- **Operating in Shared Space.** Our deeply held views do not have to be subjugated to cooperate with others, we only have to look to make as much space for their views as we want for ours.

At the end of each chapter, you'll find three suggestions you can use to practice the language of healing in your own day-to-day interactions. Choose any one of them and see how it can expand your ability to engage a wider variety of people.

We all win if you take one of the chapter topics to explore more deeply. We all win if your level of understanding increases even slightly. We all win if you take this book into a book club and have your own conversation about differences in our culture. We all win when these chapters are used as discussion starters in college classrooms or used in high school civics. We all win if you learn to listen better to people who see the world differently than you do.

The hope is that everyone who reads this will gain a little more awareness about themselves. You don't have to agree with everything here, but if you can at least acknowledge the validity of varying perspectives and communicate about them more generously, you can help repair the rip in our societal fabric. Just maybe something you read will encourage you to more harmony and peace with your family, colleagues, and friends. Even better, you may learn something here that will give you the insight to solve a problem or repair a broken relationship.

Polarity damages people. The current atmosphere is saturated with disdain for one another. It's time for a new approach that celebrates our common humanity.

"You can safely assume you've created God in your own image when it turns out that God hates all the same people you do."

— Anne Lamott

SECTION 1

An Opportune Moment

The country appears hopelessly polarized by media and political parties. Fortunately, there are only a few people who profit from the divisive climate of our nation. There are an increasing number of people who are tired of the paralysis of government and the rancor of the dialogue.

There has never been a better time for us to learn how to communicate more effectively with the people in our lives, especially those with whom we have significant disagreements. It will revitalize old friendships and open doors to new ones. We don't have to agree with each other to explore better avenues of mutual respect and cooperation.

1

A Fork in the Road

Are you tired of all the animosity in our national dialogue? Are you sick of every mention of religion or politics among family and friends that leaves you divided and angry? Have you had enough of social media exchanges that divide us into two hostile camps on every issue, with each side's proposed solution so completely exaggerated as to be unrealistic?

We hope you are. So are we! We are three regular Americans who are convinced that our current course is not only paralyzing our national dialogue, but also destroying our social fabric. We're looking for others who want to change the conversation from the rhetoric of polarization to a language of healing, where honest differences don't have to destroy relationships and where we can find common ground through mutual respect and compassion.

"We can't sell this book." The publishing executive shook his head at me like I should have known better. It was 2003 and I was pitching a book called *When World Views Collide*, which dealt with cultural conflicts, primarily in our national political dialogue.

"Books on peacemaking don't sell," he continued, "but if you will choose a side in the fight and vilify the other, we can move that book." Remember this was the heyday of Rush Limbaugh,

Michael Moore, and Bill O'Reilly, and their diatribes against political enemies were overwhelming best-sellers. Animosity sells well; it always has.

That book never got published. Almost two decades later, we approach a critical fork in the road in our national dialogue. Will we continue to degenerate into a cacophony of angry voices unable to legislate or negotiate with one another, or will we find a different language that allows us to cultivate avenues of cooperation beyond our deepest differences? I'm hopeful the tide has turned. Most people I talk to are tired of the paralysis and polarization of our divisive national politic and how that has filtered into the inability of friends and family to discuss important issues without angry and bitter feelings.

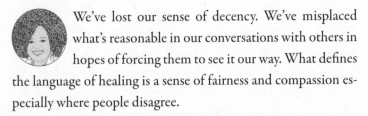 We've lost our sense of decency. We've misplaced what's reasonable in our conversations with others in hopes of forcing them to see it our way. What defines the language of healing is a sense of fairness and compassion especially where people disagree.

Reasonable is a great word. It means we can reason together, looking for the best way to solve our mutual concerns. That's at the heart of peacemaking: The word itself sets up a dichotomy. It starts with peace, which suggests passive tranquility, but that peace has to be of our making, which is active. We won't find peace if we don't take action; the peacemaker has to be on the offensive. My definition of peace may not be the same as someone whose experiences have been different than mine, whether those differences are along racial, gender, geographic, or religious lines.

Making peace doesn't mean we'll all make nice and get along perfectly. The language of healing doesn't require us to always agree, it simply opens a door to communicate graciously and find solutions that are fair for all of us. Our nation's highest hopes are not built on a shared world-view, but on mutual respect for our differing views as we build an environment where they won't divide us.

By speaking a different language, you will have the ability to explore, discover, listen, learn, and grow with an appreciation for views unlike our own. This language can help you embrace the rich tapestry of humanity and find a way to enjoy others, even beyond our disagreements.

 It reverses our tribal instincts, doesn't it? I am dismayed when people are so quick to fall into lockstep with charismatic leaders of any political or religious stripe, who have developed an uncanny ability to build their power by vilifying others. Nothing seems to unite us like a common enemy.

I didn't think that I'd ever see people who identify as spiritual, blindly entering the fray saying, "Whatever it takes to get our way, we're willing to go along." Yet that is the reality, as phrases like, "Just shut up and sing," have morphed into, "Just shut up." I was recently instructed by a friend to "stay in my lane" as a white man and stop talking about racial injustice in society. Trust me, it wasn't the first time I heard that; it won't be the last.

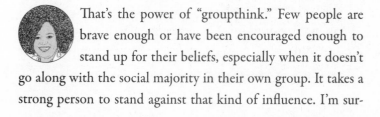 That's the power of "groupthink." Few people are brave enough or have been encouraged enough to stand up for their beliefs, especially when it doesn't go along with the social majority in their own group. It takes a strong person to stand against that kind of influence. I'm sur-

prised you two would invite me into this conversation.

 In my experience, it has been difficult to get conservatives like me to the table. Many have seen themselves as the majority voice for so long that they see many recent changes in society as a sign of their failure. I worked for twenty-five years with BridgeBuilders, a mediation and consulting service that helped bring diverse people together to cultivate the common ground. I was involved with school districts, local governments, and businesses in various forms of crisis. Those who were convinced of their own rightness were the hardest to bring to the table.

So, how do we move together as a society if we can't stake out a common ground from which we can negotiate those differences? I have found that a vast majority of people are reasonable enough to have the conversation we're suggesting. The problem is the microphones are in the hands of those who are on the extremes, who have something to gain from exacerbating the conflict, rather than resolving it.

Learning a New Language

 In my lifetime, the language of animosity has become an art form. I hadn't heard the term *fake news* before 2015. Today it's everywhere. Those two simple words have become a way of dismissing anything we find uncomfortable, and it also keeps us in a constant stalemate. Forward movement becomes impossible.

I am finding great value in speaking and writing through the filter of a different language, and a richer life spending time with people where that language is well spoken.

●

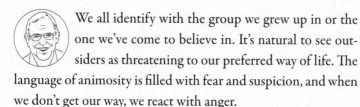 We all identify with the group we grew up in or the one we've come to believe in. It's natural to see outsiders as threatening to our preferred way of life. The language of animosity is filled with fear and suspicion, and when we don't get our way, we react with anger.

The language of healing makes room for these differences without that fear. It's not just civility for civility's sake. It is a genuine awareness that my group doesn't have all the wisdom, nor will it alone create the environment in which others can flourish. Those who have different experiences and cultures will have ideas that can benefit us if we choose to be exposed to them.

For that, we need a new language, one void of judgment and animosity. If I want to go to Paris someday, wouldn't it enhance my experience if I spoke their language? Not only could I easily navigate the city, my interactions with others would broaden. What if we learned a different way to communicate that opened new doors to understanding one another?

If you're looking for more capacity in your personal life, learning another language will help accomplish that. When I learned French, the process of conjugating verbs and learning sight words was difficult. It took time, but I learned to appreciate the process.

In 2012, the Swedish Army conducted a study with MRI scans taken before and after the exercise of learning a new language. After an intense, concentrated course designed to shorten the time ordinarily needed to become proficient in a new language, scans revealed that the areas of the brain associated with learning had actually grown in size. Learning a language increased the mental capacity for all learning and may help the brain resist dementia.

I've enjoyed learning this new language. Others around me were more proficient at it: It takes practice. Don't be afraid to make mistakes and have fun when you do. I started out using it intentionally, and eventually it has become second nature.

Proximity Is Pivotal

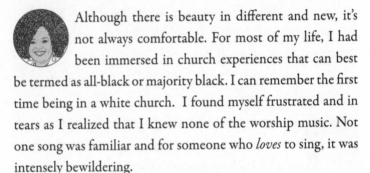

Although there is beauty in different and new, it's not always comfortable. For most of my life, I had been immersed in church experiences that can best be termed as all-black or majority black. I can remember the first time being in a white church. I found myself frustrated and in tears as I realized that I knew none of the worship music. Not one song was familiar and for someone who *loves* to sing, it was intensely bewildering.

I chose to stay anyway and during my time there, I met many wonderful people and even got to share my gifts, including singing. I would have missed all of that if I'd given in to my discomfort and never returned. Trying something new can be lonely or even painful, but the growth I've experienced has been worth the process.

One of my dearest friends is a Muslim, and for years he was the only practicing Amir in the entire United States. That means he was the legal and spiritual head of thousands of Muslims in our area. Our relationship began with a very contentious interview that I conducted for our local newspaper. Afterward, he was less than happy, but I managed to say something that made him laugh—so I took a chance and invited him to breakfast.

"Why in the world would I want to do that?" It was a contentious interview, so his answer wasn't a surprise. Even so, I smiled and said, "You should have breakfast with me simply because you should." He smiled and sighed as we exchanged numbers.

The first few minutes of our first breakfast began with religion, but I was certain that would lead to a dead end. "Did you go to school?" I asked. He replied that he had attended the University of Southern California and studied Islam with some of the top clerics in the world. I told him that I knew a few things, as well, even though my education was from a denominational school called LIFE Bible College.

I then made a request. "Tell me your story. Start at the beginning and don't leave anything out." More than three hours later, I learned that he moved to Bakersfield, California, at the age of five. I found out that his father had been involved in the ministry of trade in Kuwait. He told me the story of his dad's life being saved by Muhammed Ali. Literally. And I heard what it was like to grow up as a Muslim in Kern County—California's most conservative area. We found how much we had in common. We both loved our families. We both loved God. And we both had a passion for football. At the end, Emad said, "I recently sat with a PhD in religious studies and this conversation is far more fascinating. Could we meet again next week?"

That breakfast led to several years of relationship—including a podcast we do together called *A Christian and a Muslim Walk into a Studio*. We occasionally fight like cats and dogs over our different views, but I would give the shirt off my back to him or his family. And I know, without question, he would do the same for me. I now have a better understanding of Islamic culture. How could I not? I began to spend consistent time with someone different. As our journey has progressed, I have a better understanding of his frustrations and what he's risked in living here.

I love what you said: "I understand." Because you spend time with him, you're growing to understand him. People often won't pursue relationship without that understanding, but the only way to get it is to risk having the relationship.

And neither one of you had to sacrifice your passion or your beliefs. You didn't have to be less Christian, or he less Muslim. We can still hold passionate views while we work toward a system where we share space with people who disagree with us. I grew up in a very religious conservative environment with the understanding that we had everything right. Certain people were marginalized simply because they didn't fit our version of what was right and true. They weren't part of the home team.

My eyes were opened when I volunteered in the public school where our children attended. I was forced to engage with those who didn't share my views. To my surprise, I found them to be likeable and sincere. That changed me. I began to see that I had reached conclusions based on a very narrow set of parameters. I discovered people who came to conclusions different from mine, based on their unique experiences and circumstances. I realized that my narrow view wasn't always best or theirs always wrong. Unfortunately, the narrow scope of our experience is often exploited to force others out of the conversation, instead of expanding it to include them.

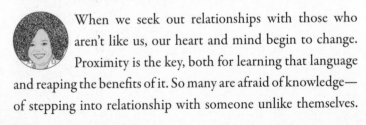 When we seek out relationships with those who aren't like us, our heart and mind begin to change. Proximity is the key, both for learning that language and reaping the benefits of it. So many are afraid of knowledge—of stepping into relationship with someone unlike themselves.

Those steps can change us—and the world around us.

Respect Doesn't Demand Agreement

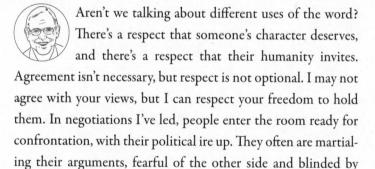

Today, disagreements make us enemies, and we advance our goals by mocking or exaggerating what others think. This is about more than the words we use; it's in our demeanor and how we treat others. If our conversation begins with the thought that "I'm right and you're wrong," we won't get far.

It's true that the language of healing is based on mutual respect, but a fixed mind-set demands agreement and is threatened by any disagreement. In a recent book discussion I hosted, most there were of the belief that respect needs to be earned. I happen to believe that respect also has to be given, simply due to our common humanity. Since God created you, you get my respect.

Aren't we talking about different uses of the word? There's a respect that someone's character deserves, and there's a respect that their humanity invites. Agreement isn't necessary, but respect is not optional. I may not agree with your views, but I can respect your freedom to hold them. In negotiations I've led, people enter the room ready for confrontation, with their political ire up. They often are martialing their arguments, fearful of the other side and blinded by their stereotypical views of them.

After a brief training on our civic compact to create an environment that offers justice and freedom for all, the dialogue changes dramatically. Instead of fighting for their way, they start looking for that common ground that allows both sides to get what they need. Your conscience may be informed differently than mine. What's important to me may not be for you. I may disagree, but I want you to have the same freedom of conscience that I want for myself. Our most difficult issues can only be navigated when we show genuine respect for points of view different than our own.

We're inviting people away from the fringes of imagined superiority, back to the middle where shared values cross diverse lines. Those who have made it their life's work to be on the fringe and grab society's power for themselves—white supremacists or antifa—will show zero interest in learning the language of healing. Those who demand that all African-Americans "go back to Africa," Muslims to their original homelands, or gays and lesbians back to their closets will find themselves uninterested or unable to change. This is a beckoning call for the vast majority in the middle to come to the fore.

Even in our opposing views, we have enough to get started if we're willing to face one another with honesty. Often, we are combating those with fixed mindsets who think they have all the facts when, in reality, they may not. We must address the thinking that says it's okay to fight forever, as long as we're on the "right" side.

You won't have the capacity to listen to others and learn from them if you're not growth minded.

Much of our conflict is based on stereotypes—exaggerations and caricatures intended to be dismissive of someone else's point of view. Both sides are guilty of comparing their best intentions with the worst examples of the other side. It's easy to get caught up in the rhetoric without realizing how much of it is fabricated and unfair.

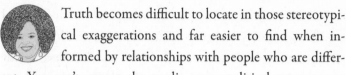 Truth becomes difficult to locate in those stereotypical exaggerations and far easier to find when informed by relationships with people who are different. You can't expect the media, your political party, or an advocate to give you an honest view of another person's perspective. Consciously relating to different people becomes the only way to debunk stereotypical thought and find out what others really think. Rarely do we find people who are willing to operate in close enough proximity to find out what's true.

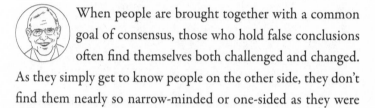 When people are brought together with a common goal of consensus, those who hold false conclusions often find themselves both challenged and changed. As they simply get to know people on the other side, they don't find them nearly so narrow-minded or one-sided as they were led to believe.

That's why we have to ask what's true, and not just blindly believe what we've been told. I can be persuasive with people and I've been cautioned several times to be careful how I lead. "You could easily be a cult leader," has been spoken to me on more than one occasion. Some people are led more by personality than by facts. I certainly believe in nuance within a story and I understand that there are different ways to tell the truth, but at its base, I see truth as an absolute.

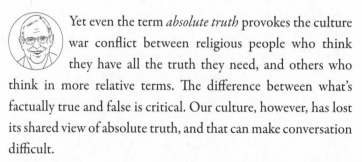 Yet even the term *absolute truth* provokes the culture war conflict between religious people who think they have all the truth they need, and others who think in more relative terms. The difference between what's factually true and false is critical. Our culture, however, has lost its shared view of absolute truth, and that can make conversation difficult.

The language of healing doesn't require us to hold the same worldviews from which we derive ultimate truth. Even those who believe in absolutes will concede that our discovery of truth is often relative to our own experience. To recognize and embrace what's true is a process that requires growth and patience. In the meantime, we can still build common ground if we champion the liberty of conscience for all.

Compromise or Consensus?

Are we talking about compromise here? Many people think that's a dirty word, when in reality it's often a path to healing. The language of healing requires us to lay down pieces of our agenda for a larger common good.

I actually see a difference between consensus and compromise. *Compromise* is trading tit for tat until we find a tolerable solution. That may be necessary at times, but when I think of *consensus,* I envision people putting their best ideas on the table and crafting a different option that both sides can embrace. That process leads to better and far more enduring solutions than those won in compromise. I always press for consensus. I've watched polarized groups walk away from the table with unanimous agreement, both feeling as if the final solution was better than what either of them brought to the meeting.

That's not possible without *collaboration.* There is power when we all come to the table. I bring what I bring. You bring what you bring. We work together to build something of mutual benefit for all when we walk away. The hope is for an equitable outcome so one party does not lose out disproportionately. Collaboration can be uncomfortable and, without doubt, reaching for it can be disruptive.

Isn't this the hard work of living in a diverse society?

If it includes everyone. I sit with many from the LGBTQ community who have a legitimate fear of being shunned or rejected outright. I often hear the words, "If people find out who I really am..." Consensus can't happen until we create a safe place for people who are different. It requires all to be represented at the table.

We each have to consciously make that choice—to stretch our capacity for relationship and insight. It will be uncomfortable for many like it was for me, but well worth the journey.

•

Try This

Crawl: *As you stand at your "fork in the road," what would most inspire you to learn the language of healing?*

Walk: *Can you think of someone you could invite to learn it with you, so you can practice with each other?*

Run: *Schedule a coffee or lunch with one person who is very different from you, that you would like to know better.*

2

What's in It for Me?

It's difficult to buck the status quo. Even if it isn't all that you hope for, it is at least predictable and you already know how to navigate it. Anything new, especially without guarantees, is always a risk. Learning the language of healing requires the courage to face the unknown and the willingness to go against the flow. And yet, some of our most impactful experiences come when we push beyond the status quo despite our reluctance.

Learning a new way to communicate with people around you, especially those with whom you hold significant differences, is not without its risks and rewards. But is it worth it? Let's find out.

In the personal and leadership coaching world, we challenge people to try something new. A good coach understands that the motivation to do so is imperative. Many times, they ask why they should. "What's in it for me?" "How can I benefit from the new thing?" As we invite you to embark on a journey of learning a new language of healing, we want to help you answer that question.

That will help carry you through the challenges of becoming proficient in the language of healing. There's a reason most of us stay to our own groupings and find it easier to criticize others than to truly understand them.

Perhaps the most significant benefit is that you'll learn to expand your comfort zone. Admittedly this is a two-sided coin. We like our comfort zones. It's easy to stay with people who think like us, talk like us, and look like us. We know how to get along and we can avoid offending people. It's a bit unnerving to meet with new people who don't necessarily embrace the same views I do. What if I say something others find offensive? What if the people in that new group don't like me, or don't accept me? Such discomfort keeps us clinging to our regular routines.

Facing the Cost

I've experienced some of that. During the last few decades I've sought out connections with people who are different from me. That has brought me into the orbit of people who have been sexually marginalized in our wider culture and those relationships have come with a cost. When I talk about my love for them, my concerns for the challenges they face, and my willingness to lay down my life for them, I find myself at odds with many of the leaders of the community I grew up in.

The fear of being misunderstood can be crippling. After my first podcast with Emad on *A Christian and a Muslim Walk Into a Studio*, I received notes from people I had gone to church with throughout the years saying, "What are you doing? Who do you think you are?" My favorite was, "What fellowship has light with darkness?" Emad and I weren't embracing each other's religion; we were embracing each other's humanity.

A very close family member came to me, extremely angry, to let me know they are convinced that I love a Muslim more than my own family. Speaking a collaborative language with people who are different comes with risk, pain, and high costs. I am still trying to understand what my family could possibly be afraid of—or anyone else for that matter. When we are taught to fear people who are not like us, the result is often disengagement.

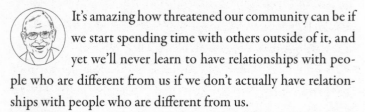 It's amazing how threatened our community can be if we start spending time with others outside of it, and yet we'll never learn to have relationships with people who are different from us if we don't actually have relationships with people who are different from us.

After spending most of our lives in African-American churches, my husband and I found ourselves attending a couple of racially homogenous white churches near our home. I had been invited to speak at a black church on a few occasions, and when people found out where I attended, I was asked, "Why are you over there?" I was viewed as a sellout or that I'd forgotten who I was and where I came from. "We could really use you over here, but you're over there."

On the flip side, in another predominantly white church there was a suspicion that I wanted something from them. Their interactions were awkward, and their unspoken questions and stares seemed to ask, "Why are you here?" "What do you want?" My only desire was to be where I thought God was leading us as a family. My goal was not to fit in, but to be a bridge.

Many years ago, I was so bothered by the racial divide in our churches, I prayed and asked God to make me a conduit of racial diversity in the local church. During the years, He has been faithful to honor my wish. When I became that conduit, I recognized that my concern for racial diversity or social justice was not a priority for most churches I attended. Painfully, I realized the sin of racism was not addressed by most spiritual leaders in the pulpit. In reflecting, the American church may not have been the best desegregation champion.

My goal has come with risk, pain, and cost. Once, a colleague asked me how it felt to be a token. I was awakened quickly! First, I was very effective in my role. Second, my personality operates very well across cultural lines and I have a high degree of cultural intelligence. So, I didn't take offense, but my feelings were hurt... a little. The question revealed more about that person than me, but the question made me realize how hard this was going to be.

Reaching beyond my comfort zone forces me to think about what I really believe, what my real core values are and what I am doing. Conflict, internal or external, can be overwhelming for some because most people do not know how to manage or resolve conflict. We don't have to be paralyzed by it. As we will see you can manage conflict through open communication, active listening, and patience.

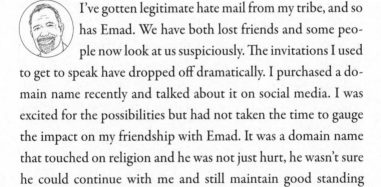 I've gotten legitimate hate mail from my tribe, and so has Emad. We have both lost friends and some people now look at us suspiciously. The invitations I used to get to speak have dropped off dramatically. I purchased a domain name recently and talked about it on social media. I was excited for the possibilities but had not taken the time to gauge the impact on my friendship with Emad. It was a domain name that touched on religion and he was not just hurt, he wasn't sure he could continue with me and still maintain good standing within the Muslim community.

It was so serious that he decided to submit the situation to the recognized ruling body for American Muslims. The council responded and asked Emad to no longer be involved with me. That led to a lunch that could have been our final time together, but I made the decision to set aside the website to honor my friend. It was an emotional time. "You would do that for me?" he asked. I assured him that I would, so he chose to proceed in our relationship. It was one of those relational moments that may never be topped. I loved him enough to set aside my own plans. He loved me enough to overlook my offense.

The Rewards of Connection

If your connections with other religions or people in the gay community bring you this much conflict from your Christian friends, why do you do it? Why do you continue to connect and pursue relationships that you know will cost you something with other relationships you value?

It is difficult to describe the level of personal satisfaction I experience by getting to know people where they are. That's what's in it for me. Giving into my fears would have changed this picture. I have become the guy who is always making new friends, whether it's the Muslim Amir or the guy taking my money in the grocery store. I've asked for phone numbers from complete strangers and been shocked when they give them to me. I build relationship by taking them to breakfast.

That's my motivation as well. Part of the delight you are experiencing is because as humans we were made for connection. Although it shocks you that perfect strangers give you their contact information, people need and desire connection. This is a major component of the language of healing. It's very human, a divine need. At the end of the day, we were put on this beautiful planet to connect with others. Society is full of people hurting and negatively acting out due to lack of connection and loneliness.

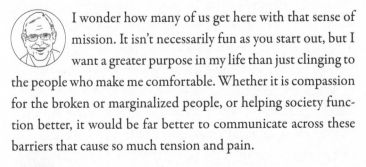

I do what I do because people are in pain and my heart has been broken for them to a point where I can't sleep well at night without actively trying to change their narrative. I choose to engage with others who are not like me because it expands my personal capacity. As I engage, I grow as a person. Everyone wants to have a voice to be heard, to know and to be known, and I'm willing to listen.

I wonder how many of us get here with that sense of mission. It isn't necessarily fun as you start out, but I want a greater purpose in my life than just clinging to the people who make me comfortable. Whether it is compassion for the broken or marginalized people, or helping society function better, it would be far better to communicate across these barriers that cause so much tension and pain.

Having the courage and ability to relate to those different from myself is a value-add to my life and a major priority. When I was a young mom of two boys, we moved to North Texas. In the first white church we attended, a small-framed Anglo-American woman caught my attention as she parented her sons. I watched her from a distance for many years as she unknowingly mentored me by proxy. I learned so much from someone so different in a place where I didn't expect it. She was my small group leader. Recently, I contacted her to let her know how much I learned from her, and she was totally shocked! Your prayers may be answered by connecting with someone different that God puts in your path.

My sincere hope is that every person who reads this book will ask themselves how learning to relate to different people adds value to their life and their children's lives.

People in need and visitors from all over the world often stayed in our home as my children grew up. They grew up with relationships with people very different from them.

A few years ago, my daughter was in the school office where her children attend, and someone who needed help came in—the demanding kind of parent that everyone else wanted to avoid. The office staff was ignoring her, so my daughter turned around and said, "Can I help you?" She was able to answer her question even though she doesn't work there. After the woman left, a school employee said, "Julie, I love the way you love people."

When she told me the story, she added, "I know where I learned to do that, Dad. I learned it from you by watching you with so many different people in our home." Hearing her say that was one of the most rewarding moments of my life.

 Intentional parenting matters. Recently, I spoke to a MOPS group about how to parent globally minded children—a sweet way of saying do not raise little racially inept ones. One person said what I so often hear, "Nobody in my family ever taught me or modeled how to engage with people different than me."

Many of them are shocked when an older family member uses a racist slur or other inappropriate comment at a family holiday meal. They don't want their kids to hear it, but a lot of our conditioning comes through our family.

 If we have to, we can use our relatives as bad examples. During his years in the Korean War, my stepfather had negative experiences with African-Americans and those experiences translated into racist thought being constantly modeled in my home. No matter how misguided, he was still my family. For the most part, I have not shielded my children from him. The dialogue became fodder for "teachable moment" conversations later. "Now you heard what Uncle John said. We do not believe that. Right?"

I admire young mothers' desire to raise their children with a more multicultural experience. Doing so opens a new world for the adults and the children. I recommend play dates with people from different cultures. More importantly, I recommend for the mom to become friends with another mom very different from herself. Close proximity to others proves to be the best way to practice the language of healing and collaboration—one new friend and one intentional act at a time.

I grew up in a tiny farming town. It was a very homogeneous community and people didn't cross boundaries socially. Now, you can't avoid the fact that we're a multicultural society. You can run from it to your own enclave, but the world around you no longer looks like you and other groups are wanting a voice at the table.

Pieces of a Puzzle

I find it amazing that some people can choose to socially select one group of people to engage for a lifetime. I don't have that luxury. White people in this society can live void of minorities, but it doesn't work the other way. I can't tell you how many people have come to my home saying, "I've never been in a black person's home before." If you don't believe me, just look at the pictures in your cell phone or who you vacation with.

I know that isn't easy to hear, but if we're going to work through the challenges of inviting diverse people to the table, it will require a certain level of humility particularly from the majority group. You must have the wherewithal, desire, and power to bring in other voices. It is just a matter of choice.

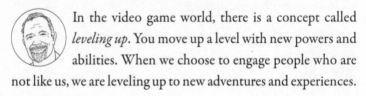

In the video game world, there is a concept called *leveling up*. You move up a level with new powers and abilities. When we choose to engage people who are not like us, we are leveling up to new adventures and experiences.

I have come to enjoy having other voices at the table. In contrast, I've been at tables void of different voices. Everybody stays in their own caricatures and stereotypes and continues to live in a narrow, colorless world. Having diverse voices and other insights from the human experience rounds out the harmony of humanity that God has put on earth. Incorporating others in our life will enrich us as people and we'll better understand our part in the whole.

In *The Gospel in Tolstoy*, Leo Tolstoy said, "I knew before that God gave life to humankind and desires that they should live. Now I understand more than that, I understand that God does not wish people to live apart and therefore he does not reveal to them what each one needs for himself, but he wishes them to live united and therefore reveals to each of them what is necessary for all." The reason we need this interconnection is because none of us have all the answers we need.

I loved *Arrival,* the movie directed by Denis Villeneuve, where alien spaceships arrive over major cities around Earth. They share twelve different pieces of a puzzle with those twelve cities, requiring humanity to cooperate to figure out why they are here. If they didn't cooperate, they would be endlessly confused. The real gift wasn't the information as much as the relationships of growing trust the aliens hope to inspire.

There are a lot of Scriptures you could draw to that same conclusion about God. God distributes gifts among the whole world. Unless we come together and collaborate, we're going to be stuck with our little pieces of the puzzle. As a result, the composite picture cannot be seen.

 If we spend time only with people like us, we miss out on so much. It is unwise for any one set of people to think they have all the answers or that their answer is *the* answer. There is no superior piece of the puzzle.

You can start to learn a language of healing by examining personal paradigms—you don't even need to know the actual outcome. It is easy to become outcome-focused and miss the graduated learning needed during the process. Sometimes your healing may come in step three. Other times, healing may come at step twenty. Please know, we're not advocating blind compliance with what we say, but we encourage individual thinking and reflection. Just walk, learn, understand, and reason with us. Be a piece of our universal puzzle.

 So, I guess the worst that can happen is you could get your world broadened. You may lose some older, weaker relationships along the way, but you will meet some people with some of the insights you have been seeking.

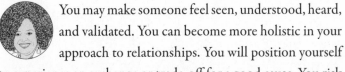 You may make someone feel seen, understood, heard, and validated. You can become more holistic in your approach to relationships. You will position yourself to experience an exchange or trade-off for a good cause. You risk misunderstanding. You risk awkwardness. You risk a lot, but it is a risk worth taking.

It's like the risk we took here. We had just met Arnita when we invited her into this collaboration. I crossed paths with her, and that connection led me to believe her wisdom and experience would add to our discussion what neither Bob nor I had. For most of us, if we just open our hearts to the people we already work with, live near, or pass by in the grocery store, our lives would be enriched.

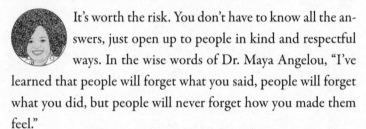 It's worth the risk. You don't have to know all the answers, just open up to people in kind and respectful ways. In the wise words of Dr. Maya Angelou, "I've learned that people will forget what you said, people will forget what you did, but people will never forget how you made them feel."

•

Try This

Crawl: *Take note of how often you mentally refer to "those people" when you're frustrated at someone's words or actions. Uncover the false stereotype behind it and find a better way to respond that won't marginalize them.*

Walk: *What assumptions do you make about others that inhibit you from finding value in relating to someone different?*

Run: *Identify three personal benefits for you in relating to someone who is different politically, socially, or religiously.*

3

Pardon Me, Your Tribe Is Showing

———————————◆———————————

Do we want to live in a society where divergent tribes fight over who can gain the most advantage for themselves through legislation and public perception, or do we want to build a society that is fair for all, despite our differences?

If we choose the latter, we will be swimming upstream against a powerful current, not only of human instinct, but also of the commercial potential derived from fomenting the very adversity that's destroying us. Tribalism shows itself almost everywhere and the question that confronts us is whether we have the courage to recognize it and move beyond it.

Tribalism served us well for most of human history. It afforded us protection from outsiders who meant us harm and allowed us to work with like-minded people and share the fruits of that labor. In one sense my extended family is a tribe. My children and grandchildren know that no matter what, I have their back.

It gives us a measure of shared experience, belonging, and connection. Tribes are great for building networks, for promoting inclusion, and for providing people a level of comfort.

We are all more comfortable with some people than others; that isn't sinister. Most of us have a natural tendency to gravitate toward people who think like us, share the same interests, or even look like us. Even business strategies encourage identifying your tribe so that you can build your brand, market to them effectively, and build a community to promote your ideas. Churches, political parties, advocacy groups, clubs, sports teams, even street gangs all are forms of seeking identity and protection inside a tribe.

That made it easy for nations to form along homogenous lines. If we all share the same language and worldview it is easier to maintain a cohesive society. But our nation was founded on a different set of ideals. It was intended to transcend our tribal instincts and build a peaceful society out of a melting pot of diverse cultures.

Unfortunately, they only saw that in terms of European culture and religious faith. They were unable to apply it toward indigenous or enslaved people. Our nation's ongoing challenge has been to apply those same ideals to the people they left out.

It has not been easy, but it is essential. Increasingly, cultures are intermingling and we will either find ways to work together beyond our differences or we will endlessly fight over who gets power. For any dominant group to hold on to power, it has to become oppressive. That's where tribalism doesn't serve us well.

The Dark Side of Tribalism

Loyalty is often a prized asset in tribal life. I've worked for people who have demanded that I act unethically, and when I protested, my loyalty to the company—the tribe—was questioned. The demand for unquestioned loyalty can be found in most tribes, whether it be political, familial, or any other. Unfortunately, it's often how churches are run and how business gets done.

I knew one man who had served as an associate pastor at a megachurch of nearly ten thousand members. After nearly fifteen years on that staff, he resigned when the senior pastor stated that the staff was not there to have any original thought or idea. They were simply tools to promote the senior leader's vision. Loyalty trumped all else, even doing what is right. Unfortunately, blind loyalty is tribalism at its absolute worst.

 Loyalty is an important component of most leadership styles, but it goes too far when you ask people to be loyal to you right or wrong. I've never bought into this perspective. I'm a student of leadership. I need people who will come against me with some friction and push back.

I wouldn't give unquestioned loyalty to anyone. I would align with my family on most things, but I don't mind disagreeing with them when circumstance demands it. I love them, but I don't necessarily support or agree with all their ideas or actions.

Yet, when a new representative goes to Washington to press for change, she finds out quickly that if she won't fall in line with the party leadership, she won't get the committee assignments she wants or the funds she needs to run for reelection. Early on, she is compromised by party power. Where loyalty to the tribe is the overriding value, truth and honesty get lost; it keeps us from growing and discovering better solutions to our problems.

I had a conversation toward the end of a presidential election with a politician who also happened to be a friend. He had come out in support of a candidate even though I knew he had major reservations about him as a person. I knew him to be a compassionate leader with whom I simply differ on many political issues. I expressed my disappointment and told him how surprised I had been. "How can you come out for someone with his level of rudeness when you love people so genuinely?" After a long conversation, he replied, "Our two-party system limits my options, Bob. Plus, I am expected to follow my party leaders. I aspire to go further politically, so, what am I supposed to do?"

I told him what I tell everybody: "Have courage!" But I certainly understood his dilemma. If he had any hope for a future in politics, he had to respect the wishes of the more powerful members of his tribe.

It takes courage and some alternative options to live beyond our tribal instincts. Tribalism is always enforced along power lines and thus is viewed very differently whether it's in the majority or minority. If you're in the majority, perhaps you use it to hoard power. If you're part of the marginalized people in the country, tribalism may be your way to survive so leaving that normal is a big deal.

The Fear Factor

Many groups find their identity by provoking fear of "the other." Instead of seeing our group as one of many, we see it as superior and find justifications for diminishing the rights and opportunities of others. Those who disagree become the enemy intent on trying to destroy the America we hold dear.

Pew Research Center—a polling force for twenty years—has been tracking polarization in politics and during the course of the last ten years, we have become more divided than ever. In

2014, they found out 44 percent of politically engaged Democrats and 51 percent of politically engaged Republicans see the other party as harmful to the well-being of our nation. They don't just have different views; the other is destructive. And that was before the ultra-divisive 2016 campaign that included Russia stoking the fire.

They found that 92 percent of Republicans are to the right of the median Democrat, and 94 percent of Democrats are to the left of the median Republican. No wonder Congress can't get anything done and why our elections are so filled with vitriol. Political tribalism has robbed us of our ability to see one another as fellow citizens.

 The animosity we have now is off the charts and we can see its impact every day. We're not making decisions for the good of the country, but instead how it will affect the power of the political parties. The party out of power has turned obstructionist, lest the other get credit and win the next election, too.

Animosity sells! There are too many people today profiting from keeping us polarized. The political parties do it to garner votes. The media does it to chase ratings and internet clicks. Much of today's journalism has clear lines of tribal affiliation, choosing the "facts" they want to tell to sustain their narrative, all the while knowing that angry conflict draws viewers. Many lobbyists and advocacy groups then further exploit that divide for their gain at some other group's expense.

The constant echo chambers of our own tribes is ripping at our social fabric. They perpetuate our fear of the "other" in twenty-four-hour news cycles and people make critical decisions based on the fear they've been sold.

Whenever we wade into the political fray willing to embrace any tactic necessary to advance our agenda, we can easily undermine our own tribe's priorities. Mark Labberton, the president of Fuller Theological Seminary, confronted fellow evangelicals with the danger of compromising their own convictions to advance their political agenda in a controversial speech at Wheaton College in Illinois. "The central crisis facing us is that the gospel of Jesus Christ has been betrayed and shamed by an evangelicalism that has violated its own moral and spiritual integrity."

If I'm honest, I've been guiltier than most. To think that those who embrace love and peace as high ideals exacerbate the division and anger that plagues our nation is unfathomable to me now.

 I was at Vanderbilt University years ago helping negotiate a policy for public schools about Intelligent Design under the auspices of Freedom Forum First Amendment Center. Could we find a way to talk about it in public schools without causing the ACLU to sue on the basis of religious indoctrination? The ACLU was there, as were scientists, educators, and creationist groups.

By the second day we were close to a solution, but the closer we got, the more recalcitrant the creationist groups became. They started pushing for changes others couldn't support. When we took a break for lunch, I pulled two of them aside to find out why they seemed to be sabotaging the agreement. One of them told me that they had come to realize that more than twenty-five organizations make their money on this fight. "If we solve it today, we'll put two hundred and fifty to three hundred people out of work. Do you want to be responsible for that?" I laughed and told him, "Of course I do!"

That's the problem we face today. No matter what the issue, people are making money or gaining political power on the fight itself. They can't afford to solve the issues because they've turned the conflict itself into profit.

In the 1960s and 1970s, it became known among fund-raisers that you could raise more funds by raising fears than you could by making an appeal for their program. Even though fund-raising responses only garnered a 2 or 3 percent response rate, that message was still in the hands of the other 97 percent. Those fears created stereotypes in our thinking that "those" people, whether it's liberals, conservatives, immigrants, evangelicals, blacks, women, or Muslims, are worthy of our fear and we must fight against them before they destroy the America we hold dear.

That fear has proved to be a powerful elixir for the past seventy years. In the 1950s, it was Communism infiltrating the United States. When the culture wars began in the 1960s, religious groups were told their faith was under attack by those who wanted God removed from society. The civil rights movement and anti-war movement only added to those fears. Now, it's LGBTQ rights, charges of racism, gun violence, and immigration issues.

I grew up in the South, Middle Tennessee, in a minority family. I was never taught racism, to hate others, or that people in a certain group were bad. Instead, I was taught there are some people you trust more than others. When we follow tribalism to a fault, it becomes important to reverse our own learned experience to unlearn some of what we've been taught. Most aren't willing to take the time, effort, or energy to do that. It is easier for them to default to their upbringing even in the face of contradictory facts. I remember going through a similar process in my spiritual walk. I decided to question traditions of men and some rote teachings in order to pursue my own faith walk at higher levels of exploring truth than what my tribe embraced.

The danger in being extremely tribal is that you fail to let other people or information come into your world. If your system is closed it will lead to toxicity. Those who speak the language of healing will want to learn and discover from the insights of others.

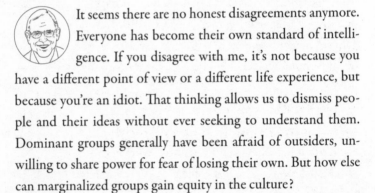 It seems there are no honest disagreements anymore. Everyone has become their own standard of intelligence. If you disagree with me, it's not because you have a different point of view or a different life experience, but because you're an idiot. That thinking allows us to dismiss people and their ideas without ever seeking to understand them. Dominant groups generally have been afraid of outsiders, unwilling to share power for fear of losing their own. But how else can marginalized groups gain equity in the culture?

The truest meaning of *conservative,* without political connotation, often becomes synonymous with a desire to keep things the way they are, or traditional. I'm convinced that our current level of negative racial polarization has a lot to do with a man of color becoming president, which was very nontraditional. In America, we never thought a descendant from Africa, and even a slave ship, would hold the power of the free world in his hands.

Reactions to that election, however, weren't all positive. Fear and suspicion of young black men increased. My conversations with moms of African-American sons changed. We were more concerned about the safety of our children and their interactions with law enforcement. I never had to talk to my kids before about surviving traffic stops, wearing hoodies, or taking non-threatening postures.

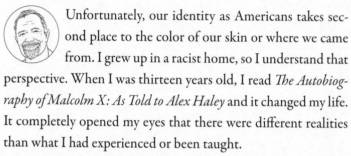

Unfortunately, our identity as Americans takes second place to the color of our skin or where we came from. I grew up in a racist home, so I understand that perspective. When I was thirteen years old, I read *The Autobiography of Malcolm X: As Told to Alex Haley* and it changed my life. It completely opened my eyes that there were different realities than what I had experienced or been taught.

Education is an important component to opening our eyes. You bring up the election of President Obama as being a catalyst for anger, at least in this country. Among the white, conservative evangelicals that I know, you are close to 100 percent right.

Moving Beyond Our Tribal Instincts

One of the ways to understand tribal thinking is to consider the dynamics of *in-groups* and *out-groups*. The group I identify with in a time and context is my in-group. Sometimes, my in-group is female. Other times, it's African-American. Sometimes it's that I'm a Christian. My out-groups are those people with whom I do not psychologically identify.

In my lifetime, I've been privileged to engage with other people's in-groups. I may have been in their out-group, but once they got to know me we could go beyond the groups we identify with.

Often, I hear "compliments" like, "Wow! You're different than all the other black women I've met." My problem with that "compliment" is, instead of thinking, "You know what, maybe I need to reexamine my stereotypes of black women," they perceive me as an outlier. I could be the opportunity for them to examine their bias. There are many black women like me, and if they had more relationships with them, they would know that.

 If we don't explore outside our in-groups, we won't have the conversations and learning opportunities we need for society to work. Psychologist Jonathan Haidt who teaches Ethical Leadership at New York University's Stern School of Business, has some hopeful research about finding our way beyond our in-group.

He identified five moral foundations that make up our humanity. The two that remain consistent across humanity are *care* and *fairness*. The others vary significantly between *race, political ideology,* and *other identifiers*. It may explain why in a crisis, we respond to human misery without any thought beyond our common humanity. Whether it's the aftermath of a hurricane in Houston or wildfires out West, people respond in overwhelming fashion to people caught in crisis without regard to their differences.

I discovered a long time ago that appealing to fairness and compassion in conflicted groups would open the door to a wider range of solutions than either side could see on their own. When people realize they don't have the right to ask for more freedom for themselves than they are willing to give others, they are able to look for the common ground.

I've often watched a member of one group argue for a point the other side would want. They recognize concerns the other group might be reticent to raise. That's what the language of healing does, in seeking to be fair to others it can change the conversation. In moving beyond our in-group, we become a bigger person, not a smaller one. The problem is almost no one is tapping that motivation.

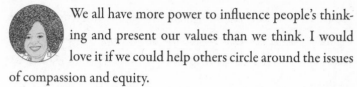 We all have more power to influence people's thinking and present our values than we think. I would love it if we could help others circle around the issues of compassion and equity.

A few years ago, I posted on Facebook a story about a mom who lost her children due to a traffic stop that went horribly wrong. Comments from many of my white friends blamed the victims. "They should have done everything the cops asked..." even though the videos showed them complying with the police. In his fear, the officer misread the situation and abused his power. The victim-shaming of my friends was so eye-opening to me! Here was a grieving mom whose kids were in a traffic stop and didn't come out alive. Where was their compassion for a fellow mom?

I particularly couldn't find that compassion in the majority of my Christian friends that make up much of my Facebook family. One of my sons reviewed the post, called me and said, "You really need some new friends, Mom." Maybe so, or perhaps I could help my current friends view this tragedy from a different perspective.

Isn't that what this tribal polarization does? It flattens an issue until there is no nuance. You either have to be completely on the side of the police or you have to see all black youth as innocent victims. It doesn't allow us to look at specific situations and realize there are bad cops and fearful ones who go too far, as well as people who act in threatening ways that compels a response no one wants.

When black athletes started kneeling during the national anthem in the NFL to raise consciousness of racial inequities, others hijacked their concerns by accusing them of disrespecting the military. By making it about something unrelated to their action, they could avoid a conversation that makes them uncomfortable. People were forced to choose between supporting our military or caring about inequities for black people. Can't we do both?

By changing their message to "all lives matter," the majority could ignore the fact that some lives seem to matter less when they still face systemic racism and undeserved suspicion. If you don't believe that, it's because you don't have meaningful connections with people who deal with it.

A Christian and a Muslim Walk into a Studio—my podcast with Emad—helps both of our communities see that fear doesn't need to be the final word. The backlash I've taken from my own Christian community has been hurtful, but I understand that there's a price to be paid when you build a bridge to one of your out-groups.

Several years ago, I discovered a feral cat lying in my flower bed. He was emaciated, angry, and near death. I couldn't get within ten feet of him, but compassion led me to bring him food and water. As he regained health, he began to claim our home as his. I named him Douglas Fur. Every day, I would feed him while speaking gently and sometimes I even sang to him. His tail would move gently when he heard my voice. After a year, he brought another feral cat to us. She was beat up, frightened, and pregnant, but he had convinced her that we were different. It's as if he had said to her, "I know we were taught to fear these people, but this one is different. Trust me, you'll see."

I get to be like Douglas Fur with those who fear Muslims, gay people, and others who are not like us. Fear is the automatic response for most, but it can be overcome by those who have stepped through.

The Most Powerful Voice at the Table

 In negotiating common ground agreements, I have found the most powerful voice at the table is not the person speaking up for their own vested interest, but the one who defends the rights of opposition when they are being crowded out of the conversation. We need more voices that stand up for the others, finding a way to fairness, compassion, and respect. We already have enough voices pushing toward fear with stereotyping and animosity. One voice can completely change the temper of a room and open the door for mutual respect and understanding.

 Many of us want to inhabit the middle ground, but there are many leaders who present political party affiliations as a litmus test. It creates an element of fear that isn't easy for most to overcome. It's the same in abortion debates. Pro-choice or pro-life. No in-between.

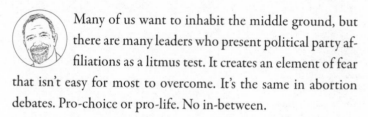 If we can overcome such either/or thinking, we would find viable alternatives. In the 2016 election we had two options presented as immigration policy: open borders and amnesty for all or build a wall and deport them all. By offering two mutually exclusive options we stifle the debate. The permutations between those two extremes might offer us a common ground solution. How can we even talk about the issue when we don't even use the same terminology? One side insists on using the phrase "undocumented workers" while the other side prefers "illegal immigrants."

 Doesn't this reflect a level of insecurity and lack of critical thinking? In future chapters, we'll see how being forced to see every issue in a binary construct limits our options to find the best solution. We must explore nuance and assume most people can think and reason.

 This is where we need reasonable people to come to the fore. While the language of healing asks us to reach across our tribal lines, that doesn't mean we can find common ground with everyone. Seeking the common ground fairly marginalizes those extremists, like white supremacists or antifa, who only want power for their own group. The process itself will leave some voices out. As Megan Phelps-Roper, a survivor of the anti-gay Westboro Baptist Church, said this about her own involvement: "I thought my rightness justified my rudeness." No, it doesn't.

 Engaging people in our out-group personally is the way to evolve beyond your stereotypes. You won't be able to understand or advocate for them until you have enough proximity to understand them.

When I look at people on a macro level, I realize we're all part of humanity. Everyone wants compassion; all people want equity; all people want to love and be loved. Let's prioritize the macro level. That's where we start. That's how I live. There are things I'm sensitive to because I wouldn't want my worst enemy to endure them.

•

Try This

Crawl: *Recognize when you deem someone in your out-group as "stupid" for not having the same views you do. Instead can you think of a good reason why they might hold those views?*

Walk: *Identify what in-groups you consider yourself a part of and what out-groups you tend to avoid. Can you see yourself learning more about an out-group?*

Run: *Invite a person in your out-group into a conversation with the intent of gaining understanding from their point of view.*

4

The Symphony of Different

There have been moments in history where those with differing agendas found the ability to work together toward a common goal.

From politicians to movie studios, we've seen agendas set aside for peace, money, and sometimes both. Perhaps there is no better example in sports than the 1992 Olympic "Dream Team." The roster representing the United States featured sworn enemies Larry Bird, Magic Johnson, and Michael Jordan. Each player had already won several NBA championships by the time the '92 Olympics rolled around and had met one another on the court multiple times with titles on the line. Larry Bird, the greatest trash-talker in history, had famously refused to even socialize with those who were not on his team.

Everything changed in 1992, as this trio took the court together at the Barcelona Olympic Games. Not only did they make history—winning every game by an average margin of nearly forty-four points—they did it by becoming consummate teammates. During their eight-game stretch, all three of them had intentionally sought to lift the games of other players on the team, resulting in fewer personal scoring opportunities. Their choice, however, to work in concert with one another caused many sports journalists to refer to the "Dream Team" as the single greatest sports team ever assembled.

Their example epitomized the concept of team over individual, *regardless of their differences. In the same way if we can find a way to work together beyond our differences, we can accomplish some incredible things.*

Music is often referred to as the universal language. It's a mystical gift that affects human emotions and changes cultures. It crosses oceans, ideologies, and even time itself without effort or difficulty. Music might be the perfect analogy for the language of healing. The Beatles are enjoyed equally in Los Angeles, Moscow, and Shanghai.

While one instrument can be enchanting, multiple instruments in concert can become transcendent. In a typical symphony orchestra, there can be as many as one hundred people playing up to fifty different instruments—nearly all with different musical parts. As rich as a melody can be, its beauty is magnified when underscored with harmony and rhythm.

It's amazing how people playing different instruments in coordination with one another can produce such a magnificent sound. It parallels what we can accomplish as we discover the value of collaboration. As with a symphony, it is important to be able to contribute your part while simultaneously listening to and blending in with others.

As we learn to collaborate and appreciate how interconnected we are, we will discover more relational harmony. Our contributions can be enhanced—not diminished—as we respect the important contributions of others. When we do, we will make the effort to understand the unique perspectives others can bring to almost any endeavor.

In high school, I saw a class on the schedule called Music Appreciation. I was so intrigued by the title I asked the instructor what it meant. She explained that appreciation involved the ability to hear all the instruments individually as well as collectively. When the brass appreciates the woodwinds, or the percussion the strings, beautiful music emerges.

There's a difference between a soloist and a musician in the orchestra. Those in the orchestra must give up their need to be the center of attention. The collective must take precedence over our own preference.

Unfortunately, rugged American individualism has taught us to value just the opposite. Society often rewards getting to the front of the line no matter the cost. To speak this language will run counter to most things we've been taught.

That's true in sports. Everyone knows Aaron Rodgers, the quarterback of the Green Bay Packers, but only diehard fans know the names of the men who put their bodies on the line to keep him safe—his offensive linemen. When you look at the quarterback standing next to an offensive lineman, you can easily see that they possess a different skill set. Rodgers understood their unheralded value, however, and rewarded them with all-terrain vehicles that cost $20,000 each. He understood that the quarterback may get the glory, but games are won or lost in the trenches.

A game is never won by a *single* player. LeBron James is one of basketball's all-time greatest, but even he has experienced defeat in the NBA Finals. The other team—usually the Golden State Warriors—was simply better. In an orchestra, a soloist can produce beauty, but eventually she sits down to contribute to the greater beauty of the whole.

●

The Power of Trust

 For a symphony to play well, the musicians have to trust one another. Its development takes both time and skill. When a culture chooses to celebrate all its participants, no matter their individual histories and journeys, we have made a choice to ascribe inherent value to everyone. Value opens the door to relationship, and relationship to trust. When we journey outside of our in-group and embrace the humanity of others, they need not threaten our existence but open new doors of understanding and cooperation.

 Without a doubt, trust is a major component of the language of healing, but not all trust is created equal. I recall a workplace situation where I could not gain the trust of a teammate. I was doing all I could to add value to the team, but she still didn't accept me. Later, I read a book by Dr. John Townsend, *Beyond Boundaries,* that helped me understand what was going on. He defined two types of trust: *Functional trust* concerns trusting someone because they are dependable. *Relational trust* refers to how safe it is to offer the other person our feelings and vulnerability.

They are not the same. It is easier for me to find functional trust for those I work alongside. That trust is not dependent on a personal relationship with them. It's simply trusting that each will do their part. You don't need to like someone to realize they have a part to play. Singing "Kumbaya" is not necessary to understand that someone else brings a different skill set to the task at hand.

Relational trust, on the other hand, is built upon a bond that moves beyond function. I know you have my back, not because it's your job, but because I know you in a more intimate manner.

Relational trust is what prompted Aaron Rodgers to buy those ATVs for his linemen. Understanding the difference between functional and relational trust gave me permission to build my relationships differently.

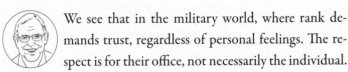

Each of us goes through life making decisions about whom to trust, hopefully doing what we can to present ourselves to others as trustworthy. We all hope for that in relationships, which is why betrayal or selfish actions are so destructive to both types of trust. If I'm not faithful enough to fulfill my promise, or if I stab someone in the back for my own gain, the damage is long-lasting.

While respect is critical for relational trust, it isn't for functional trust. We can work together with someone we don't respect. In a symphony, it is certainly possible to play with those for whom we have little respect. As long as people are true to the overriding mission, it doesn't matter if we like them or not.

We see that in the military world, where rank demands trust, regardless of personal feelings. The respect is for their office, not necessarily the individual.

Outside such hierarchical settings, however, someone's contribution opens the door for their involvement. If you can bring insight, beauty, or texture, you add value. Recognizing the inherent value of others' contribution, especially when it's different from mine, will add to the beauty not the cacophony.

Moral issues seem to confuse the symphony image here. When we have moral differences with others, it is easy for us to claim the high ground and seek to exclude those who don't agree. For instance, those who want to impose their religious views on society as a whole will not see value in adding the LGBTQ community to the symphony. Just the opposite—they find value in excluding them. The symphony of different, however, looks for contribution even beyond our differing views of morality. It's imperative to invite all people into the process.

Many see that as a contradiction, but perhaps no group of humans have contributed more to the artistic beauty of human society than the LGBTQ community. From Leonardo da Vinci to Elton John, they have added to the world's treasure and shared honest glimpses into the divine.

Morality is a difficult issue to discuss. I conducted an informal Facebook crowdsourcing poll and was amazed at the differences in how people define morality. Some see it as an absolute, often based on Scripture; others see it as more relative or based on their feelings; and another group based it on people's social reactions. My personal morality matters. It requires me to stop talking, stop assuming, and start practicing being a better listener and observer.

In the end, we are not as divided on morality as it may appear. Virtually everyone wants laws against murder, rape, assault, fraud, theft, and the like. We are most divided on sexual issues. Those who believe in absolutes as I do are free to practice our morality without imposing it on others.

If I were a judge sitting behind the bench, robed, with a gavel in my hand, and a family member was brought before me, the law would require that I recuse myself. I'm too close to the defendant to accurately dispense justice. When we allow ourselves to be close to those who are not like us, we are no longer able to function as their judge and jury.

Relationship dismantles judgment and overcomes the differences between us. Dan Reynolds, the lead singer of a group called Imagine Dragons, made a documentary called *Believer*. He is a Mormon from Utah who was touched by that state's epidemic of teen suicides, which are largely related to the Mormon Church's stance on LGBTQ issues. He revealed that the vast majority of Mormons simply want to love those who are different but are too frightened to spend time with them or speak out on their behalf, due to the very real threat of excommunication.

Fear is a powerful tool to keep people in line. Many of us face this in social media where our own "friends" serve as watchdogs to keep our thoughts in line.

Learning to PLAY

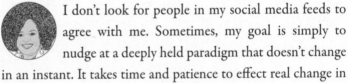 I don't look for people in my social media feeds to agree with me. Sometimes, my goal is simply to nudge at a deeply held paradigm that doesn't change in an instant. It takes time and patience to effect real change in people's long-held beliefs. We can celebrate progress, even when it arrives in smaller increments than we hope for.

Wouldn't it be great if we could PLAY together like an orchestra:

- **Purpose** to contribute your individual best to the whole relationship of your orchestra, tribe, or society.
- **Leverage** your current networks to spread the language of healing.
- **Accept** that learning to appreciate something different will cause personal discomfort.
- **Yield** your heart and mind to the new sound and discover the composite beauty of working with others.

I recently spent an evening with a group of friends on a deck in Raleigh, North Carolina, where the conversation turned to immigration. Most were hard-liners in favor of a harsh law-and-order stance regarding immigrants who are here illegally. I told a story about a friend of mine who had years earlier crossed our southern border in fear for his life because he would not join the local cartel. His story is both emotional and inspirational.

The following day, I received an email from a man who had been involved in that discussion: "For as long as I can remember, my thoughts on immigration have been very 'Republican.' Yet after last night's conversation, there's no way I can hold to the same views. Perhaps the best takeaway I had from last night is that I walked away more human."

Isn't that the goal? If we can find ways to simply be more human, hearts and minds can be changed. When we learn to acknowledge another person's struggle, experience, gifts, or viewpoint, we can better appreciate the symphony of different.

•

Try This

Crawl: *When you share your thoughts with people who think differently from you, do not communicate as if your view is the most salient perspective. Think of yours as one of many.*

Walk: *Never assume you or anyone else can accurately guess someone else's motives. It is the easiest way to unjustly smear others, so you can dismiss them. Ask yourself how you'd hear people differently if you assumed their motives were honorable?*

Run: *Identify three examples this week where you could appreciate someone's insight or actions that you have previously dismissed because they are different from yours.*

5

Staking Out the Common Ground

---◀▶---

Many think they find common ground when they can convince enough people to agree with them so they can get their way. They view the world through polarized lenses, with each issue offering two opposing and mutually exclusive options—one right the other wrong. Of course, they think themselves on the side of right and look on those who disagree with disdain.

The common ground, however, is not where we all agree, but where we map out an environment in which we can discuss our differences with mutual respect and seek a solution that is fair to those differences. That's why our Founders established our nation not as a democracy but a Democratic Republic. Thomas Jefferson pointed out why: "A democracy is nothing more than mob rule, where 51 percent of the people may take away the rights of the other 49 percent."

The higher aspirations of our "more perfect union" is to find that common ground where the rights of all are respected and the liberty of all protected. Nowhere is that needed more than where we disagree on critical issues. That may be unthinkable in an age of polarizing politics, but that only makes it a nobler pursuit.

 Finding common ground beyond significant differences was necessary from the very inception of our Republic. Thirteen disparate colonies came together to map out a common future, and to do that they had to work through political, religious, and economic differences to sort out what a government based on liberty would look like. They knew the tyranny of monarchy, where people were commanded to serve at the whim of one; and the dangers of democracy, where a slight majority could inflict great damage on the minority.

When they summoned a nation to throw off the constraints of the largest military power of their day, they needed overwhelming majorities in each colony willing to risk both life and fortunes to stake out "a new nation, conceived in liberty." To pen the Declaration of Independence, and ultimately the Constitution, required those colonies to stake out enough common ground to become a nation worth fighting for. You don't go to war on a 51 percent vote or write that kind of policy on a 5 to 4 judicial decision. These early documents resound with the language of shared ideals and shared destinies despite their differences.

By seeking to build an overwhelming majority they were forced to craft ideals that have stood the test of time and are being extended to people they excluded. Their example has all but been forgotten today. No matter what issues we face in our national politics, our neighborhoods, our families, our economic welfare, and in our ethnic and cultural differences, we should ask ourselves if we can step back and stake out a solution that embraces our differences, rather than one that only sides with a certain subset of the population.

There was no common ground for my ancestors. We weren't even regarded as human.

You can only reach common ground when everyone is at the table. The fact that blacks didn't count as people and that indigenous people were dismissed as "savages" is a grave stain in our history. The common ground they reached was for European colonists of different class, culture, and religion. Their ideals were powerful, their application was definitely flawed.

 Didn't those agreements completely unravel in the centuries since? Less than one hundred years later, we fought a horrible war over slavery. Then we fought over extending the right to vote for women, civil rights to African-Americans, and whether gay people can live without discrimination.

 Some might view it that way, but the ideals remain intact. They didn't have the vision to implement those ideals for everyone and unfortunately punted on the most significant issue that confronted the young republic—slavery. They couldn't find a workable option given the times. So, in launching a nation of liberty they carelessly denied it to a significant group of the population. We paid a severe price not a hundred years later, and still suffer its effects today.

But the more glorious heritage is that those documents set a trajectory for our nation's laws to expand those ideals to ever-widening groups of people. They are still making us a better nation, though not nearly fast enough.

Finding a Purpose Greater than Our Differences

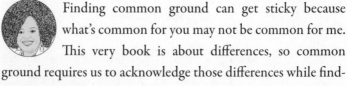 Finding common ground can get sticky because what's common for you may not be common for me. This very book is about differences, so common ground requires us to acknowledge those differences while finding our shared purpose.

No matter what differences we have we can almost always step back and find a larger issue where we can stake out a common ground. I've been in conflicted rooms arguing about policies to protect the LGBTQ community from discrimination and bullying. Many people see those attempts as undermining their moral views. But isn't the larger issue ensuring that the campus is a safe place for all staff and students? Anti-discrimination is not predicated on us holding common moral views, but in creating a safe environment for all even if we view the moral questions differently.

 Many who came to the colonies in those early days did so to escape persecution in Britain. They were willing to overlook their differences for the sake of a shared purpose.

 In the end, yes. But most spread out into homogenous communities and often persecuted those who were different. We all have our preferences and would love for the society we live in to skew toward those preferences. But the end result is always oppression for those who don't share them. This is where reasonable people—who are tired of the deep rancor of adversarial engagement—can come together and craft a common ground where we fight for fairness for all, not just for people who think like I do.

In my experience working through these conflicted issues, I found about 12 to 15 percent of people on either extreme want everyone forced to do what they think is best. Unfortunately, those are the voices we hear at school board meetings or read in letters to the editor or internet comments. However, that leaves more than 70 percent who are willing to seek a solution that is fair to others. If we can tap those reasonable people in the middle, we can define that shared purpose. Give them a platform and they will find a fair solution for everyone.

 Consensus is hard work. Building a coalition is a different process where people promote their agenda until they can take advantage over others to get what they want. Consensus requires people to accept that a decision has to be made and that the best way to approach it is to invite reasoned discussion that invites a variety of perspectives. Finally, participants have to have a sense of deference where they realize that they may not get all or most of what they want.

 That's why we need all the stakeholders in the room to make a just decision. One of the things we'd always ask before we started was, "Who have we left out?" In one school district where we were making decisions for a high school, we discovered that no students were in the room. When you leave people out, you're just imposing a solution, you are not building a common good.

Once you have the right stakeholders, you can begin the search for a shared purpose through dialogue and research. If we're all committed to a safe campus, for instance, you have to ask what it is that makes our campus unsafe. Who feels threatened and why? That's where many eyes are opened to see problems they didn't even know existed.

Then this becomes the critical question: How do we find a solution that can encompass a super-majority in the room? I often started my mediation sessions by saying, "We will be done tonight when 90 percent of us agree on a solution." Many would laugh thinking that it was my opening joke. They soon realized it wasn't and that by seeking such a broad-based solution, they had to look beyond the us-versus-them stereotypes to possibilities none of them had previously considered. In the end, we may only get 70 to 80 percent but that will still provide a better answer as well as a process that will tap a generosity of spirit that benefits the community.

Confronting Social Power

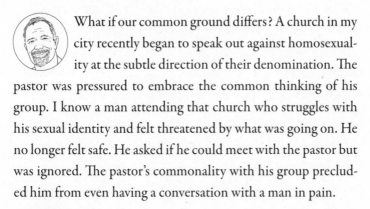

What if our common ground differs? A church in my city recently began to speak out against homosexuality at the subtle direction of their denomination. The pastor was pressured to embrace the common thinking of his group. I know a man attending that church who struggles with his sexual identity and felt threatened by what was going on. He no longer felt safe. He asked if he could meet with the pastor but was ignored. The pastor's commonality with his group precluded him from even having a conversation with a man in pain.

It seems so simple to have "just" a conversation, but the bigger issue is that he's giving in to the social powers around him that would frown upon it. You are describing the concept of social power. The pastor does not want to be linked with that person because he doesn't want the scrutiny of his social environment. We have a similar dynamic with race. Some white people will not talk to black people in certain contexts; some Latino people will not talk to Asians, and I could go on.

By giving in to social power, we avoid the conversations that may drive us to deeper reflection and reconsideration of our values and beliefs.

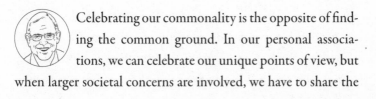

Celebrating our commonality is the opposite of finding the common ground. In our personal associations, we can celebrate our unique points of view, but when larger societal concerns are involved, we have to share the culture with people who don't agree with us. Common ground is the place where people who think differently can find a safe environment that respects those differences.

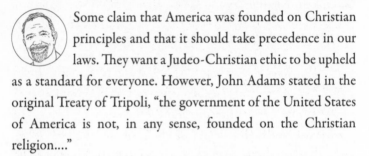 Some claim that America was founded on Christian principles and that it should take precedence in our laws. They want a Judeo-Christian ethic to be upheld as a standard for everyone. However, John Adams stated in the original Treaty of Tripoli, "the government of the United States of America is not, in any sense, founded on the Christian religion...."

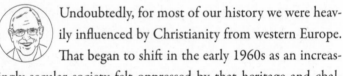 Undoubtedly, for most of our history we were heavily influenced by Christianity from western Europe. That began to shift in the early 1960s as an increasingly secular society felt oppressed by that heritage and challenged the government's role in promoting it. Interestingly enough, the Founders had already provided a solution, even if it had been previously ignored.

The First Amendment offered a way to handle religious differences and competing claims to ultimate truth. Many of the colonies had an embedded religious element, often collecting taxes to promote one sect and persecute others. Roger Williams was one of the first to see that no human government could be entrusted with religious power. He came to America after eleven successive monarchy changes in England—the monarch switched religion from Catholic to Anglican and back again to serve his or her personal interests. Each time they forced the citizens to change as well, often under penalty of death.

Williams challenged his own Puritan community by telling them they lived on stolen land and that they did not have the right to demand non-Puritans among them to live to their morality. Doing so, he termed "the rape of the soul." It wasn't even a benefit to the Puritans themselves. Forcing people to live beyond the scope of their conscience wouldn't endear them to his faith; it would only alienate them. That conviction got him exiled from the Puritan colony in the dead of winter. He ended up in Rhode Island, bought land from the native Americans, and founded a colony based on the liberty of conscience. He knew that if he wanted the freedom to live his convictions, he needed to give freedom to others to live theirs.

It was the first colony that encouraged freedom of religion, even allowing Jewish people to build their own synagogue. When the Founders dealt with religious differences in the colonies, they drew handily from his thoughts. The First Amendment restricted the government from promoting faith or undermining its practice. Though it only applied to the Federal government initially, eventually people came to see it as the only practical solution to religious conflict in state government as well.

Rather than finding religious peace through compromise, they stepped back far enough to realize they didn't have to choose between Christian, Jewish, Muslim, or atheist. By upholding the value of a liberty of conscience for all, they found a way for people of different religions, or none at all, to live side-by-side without the preference of the state. That has stood the test of time. Throughout history there has never been an example of religious faith and government power combined in the same entity that's either been good for the religion or the government. Our Founders knew if you commingle these two into a monolithic power, it will work to the oppression of others.

Remember, We Are All Human

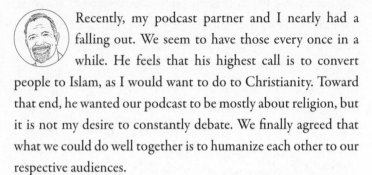 Recently, my podcast partner and I nearly had a falling out. We seem to have those every once in a while. He feels that his highest call is to convert people to Islam, as I would want to do to Christianity. Toward that end, he wanted our podcast to be mostly about religion, but it is not my desire to constantly debate. We finally agreed that what we could do well together is to humanize each other to our respective audiences.

During Ramadan one afternoon, I invited him to sing the song "Afternoon Delight" on the air after he mentioned that Muslims must fast from sex as well as food. It was hilarious, our audience was excited about two people of different faiths finding common ground. We're both men living in the United States. Think about it—we sang about sex! And guess what? We have that in common, too.

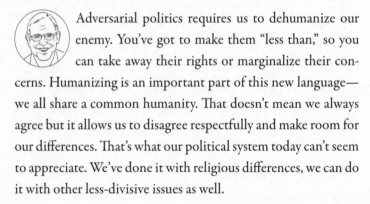 What you did, Bob, made your in-group the whole of humanity. Understanding commonness and respecting difference is the essence of the language of healing. Diversity is actually holding both of those things in tension.

Adversarial politics requires us to dehumanize our enemy. You've got to make them "less than," so you can take away their rights or marginalize their concerns. Humanizing is an important part of this new language—we all share a common humanity. That doesn't mean we always agree but it allows us to disagree respectfully and make room for our differences. That's what our political system today can't seem to appreciate. We've done it with religious differences, we can do it with other less-divisive issues as well.

The beauty of your relationship with Emad is that you're not just seeing the world through your point of view. You can also view it from his, and though it doesn't minimize your differences, it will allow you to treat them more generously.

As members of the human race, we share so much in common—our love for spouses and children, our hopes and dreams, and even our challenges. Our shared experiences transcend ideology. They are human at their core and we all hold them dear and sacred, even if we do so in different ways.

We all want to be valued by others. We all need provision. We all need love and security. We all want affirmation and acceptance. This is the place to search for common ground.

Emad and I took the Myers-Briggs personality test together on the air during one of our episodes. It was a revelation! We found out that we were *exactly* the same personality type, with one small exception. Where I perceive, he often judges. When the test asked about fitting in at work, Emad told me he once went out with coworkers and sang Christmas carols, even though he doesn't celebrate the holiday. I was taken aback, but immediately he began to sing "Silent Night." Right out loud.

I love it when our common humanity invites us to risk the social power designed to keep us with our own. Once during lunch, I asked a coworker specifics around her Christmas holiday. She paused and told me she was Muslim, though she didn't seem offended by my question. I realized the error of my assumption and quickly moved to another topic. I think she was relieved I had not judged her.

A short time after this interaction, she was sad and approached me to ask if I would pray for her! What an honor! The honest mistake I made in December paved the way for a deeper connection in March. Obviously, both of us recognized our common ground: God.

 My first thought when you said that you asked her how she celebrates Christmas, was how you react when somebody wants to touch your hair.

 I am more than my hair! A great aspect of learning the language of healing is risking relating to someone about whom you have limited cultural intelligence. Honestly, I never looked at her ethnicity and thought, "Oh, she's Muslim." I understood she was born in Northern Africa. I had just enough sensitivity and cultural intelligence to know what I had done. I could read her nonverbals. Because of her generosity, we were able to navigate through it and build a good working friendship. We later talked about more personal topics like her children being bullied and terrorized in public school for their religion. I know both of us found areas of common ground like being a mother, working outside the home, and other family concerns. We learned from each other.

The Challenges of Common Ground

 Even through differing claims to ultimate truth, it is possible to build common ground if we can step back far enough to discover what serves us all well. But I realize not every issue lends itself to that. Some issues only have two mutually exclusive options, though they are rare. We've been fighting for fifty years about abortion rights. Most religious people would prefer to outlaw them, but many on the left see them as a necessary, if not problematic, solution to a desperate situation. I've often wondered what if we'd taken all that energy we use to fight over their legality and worked together to make abortions unnecessary through education, health services, and adoption.

Perhaps the most difficult place to find the common ground is when we are dealing with historic inequities. It's easy for those who have power in the status quo to think the common ground comes from just being equitable today. What if inequity, however, has already been built into our structures like the residue of apartheid in South Africa, racial inequality in America, or centuries of conflict that plague the Middle East. These issues require even a further step back to find the solutions that encompass those inequities. What's difficult here is that often the current generation doesn't feel like the oppressor and are rarely willing to contribute to a solution.

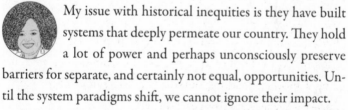 My issue with historical inequities is they have built systems that deeply permeate our country. They hold a lot of power and perhaps unconsciously preserve barriers for separate, and certainly not equal, opportunities. Until the system paradigms shift, we cannot ignore their impact.

Recently, I watched an episode of *What Would You Do?* that illustrates the problem. The show set up a scene in a local sandwich shop. The crew set up a tip jar at the front counter of a restaurant and sent in three people, one at a time, to order sandwiches. After the employee took the order and had turned their back, the "patrons" took part of the money needed to pay for their order out of the tip jar. The other customers watched them do it. The show wanted to record the patrons' responses to each individual. Inevitably, the white female got away with stealing most often without being confronted. She was only confronted a third of the time. The black male was confronted two-thirds of the time. The Muslim male was confronted almost one hundred percent of the time.

All of them were stealing money out of the same tip jar to pay for their sandwich. Why was the response so different? Inequity. We need to be honest enough to say it exists, before we can address it more effectively.

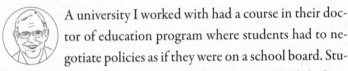 A university I worked with had a course in their doctor of education program where students had to negotiate policies as if they were on a school board. Students were assigned to the groups with whom they had the least in common—men were assigned to women's issues and liberals to the conservative religious group. People were mixed up by ethnicity, religion, special interests, and politics. They underwent training in their assigned group and would be graded on how well they could represent someone else's point of view.

The impact on students was dramatic in their assessment of differing views. Many of them came to appreciate others' concerns and realized that just because they disagreed with them, that didn't make them stupid or ill-informed. They saw how the experiences and beliefs of others were consistent within their own worldview. It broadened their capacity to listen and to care for other people.

 Calling something stupid is usually a reaction or judgement to something we do not understand. The thought of calling someone else stupid should make me step back and ask myself why I'm doing this. If I really do not understand them, why would I make a value judgment on the situation? Thinking someone stupid is the first step to dehumanizing them.

●

Try This

Crawl: *Instead of dismissing others, thinking them less than you, find ways to ask for more information to help you understand them. Use phrases such as these: "What I hear you saying is..." This will help decrease your need to be defensive.*

Walk: *Take a long look at someone you tend to treat dismissively because of the way they look or think. How can you begin to reach out to them as a fellow human being?*

Run: *Think about how society is unfair to a minority person you know. What could you do to bring more equity to the person you know?*

SECTION 2

Five Practices of a Peacemaker

Speaking the language of healing isn't a matter of semantics alone; it's also a matter of developing your character. When we are more at peace with ourselves, we will not be threatened by those who have different perspectives or beliefs. In fact, they can add to our own experience and enrich it.

Then we can work for a more generous public square, wanting others to enjoy the same benefits of a free society that we want for ourselves.

Here are five practices you can cultivate in your own character that will enable you to speak the language of healing.

6

Being Comfortable in Your Own Skin

Mark Twain said, "The worst loneliness is to not be comfortable with yourself."

Brené Brown seems to agree. "True belonging only happens when we present our authentic, imperfect selves to the world, our sense of belonging can never be greater than our level of self-acceptance."

The art of self-acceptance—being comfortable in our skin—is a skill that requires the ability to adapt as we live life. Sadly, many never acquire the proper skills necessary to navigate. Well, maybe most don't. For those who are willing to make the investment in themselves, life becomes a richer and more rewarding experience.

The other night I was wide awake at 2:30 am, which is odd for me. After I managed to pull the television remote out of its hiding place under my husband's side, I flipped through five or six channels, surprised that *every* channel had an infomercial related to skin care! There was a special product to remove a spot, kill acne, dim a scar, erase wrinkles, smooth stretch marks, help you find the right foundation color, moisturize, and cleanser. I could go on and on. They did!

Apparently, we are a culture preoccupied with skin. We are captivated by it. We want it to look flawless, and it seems we need a lot of help to make it look that way. Unfortunately, that's often true in the metaphorical sense as well. When we talk about those who are comfortable in their own skin, we aren't talking about their physical appearance, but about those who know themselves, value who they are, and present themselves to others authentically. People like that understand their abilities or the lack thereof, and they don't look to others for validation. All of these are important traits to any who wish to learn the language of healing.

I grew up in middle Tennessee, where the color of your skin was a big deal. A few years ago, I found myself on the tiny island of St. Thomas where I accompanied my husband on a work assignment. Here, I encountered a different kind of exclusion. I enjoyed being around so many people of color—and I mean all shades of color. Beautiful! And, even though my skin was the proper shade to grant me some level of inclusion, it didn't work out that way. I noticed I was being called a "Yankee" and my son, "a little Yankee." The inflection in their voices clued me in to the derogatory nature of the nickname. It meant I was from the United States, simply American.

I wasn't being excluded for my skin color this time, but for the way we talked and where we were from. Moments like this can drive us back into insecurity and withdrawal, or they can motivate us to embrace more of our personal uniqueness and thereby demolish that insecurity. I chose the latter. You can, too, as part of your personal and relational growth.

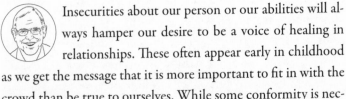 Insecurities about our person or our abilities will always hamper our desire to be a voice of healing in relationships. These often appear early in childhood as we get the message that it is more important to fit in with the crowd than be true to ourselves. While some conformity is necessary for social order, it cannot be at the expense of someone's

true self. The process of being comfortable in our own skin invites us to challenge these insecurities and discover and appreciate who we really are and the contributions we can make to others around us.

 When we're insecure, we often look for ways to bring people down to our level as a functioning mechanism. That was certainly the case for me. Encouraging words were few and far between where I grew up. In fact, it was frequently the opposite of encouragement. My insecurities ran wild as a child and those continued well into my adult life. I could always offer a witty remark under the guise of humor and sarcasm that would tear others down. Sadly, very little was off limits when I would launch into those passive-aggressive attacks. The old saying that misery loves company was true in my case. I saw myself as so lacking that I needed to make others feel the same way. The journey to undo all of that has been painful and glorious all at the same time.

Finding Our Way to Genuine

 Before we can speak the language of healing, we must embrace a process of healing ourselves before assisting others. The goal is authenticity—to become truly genuine from the inside out.

 That is truly the opposite of projecting an image, especially trying to convince people I've got it all together and I'm right about everything. Years ago, when I was writing for *Leadership Journal,* my editors taught me to always begin an article with a personal failure or struggle on that particular topic. I learned the valuable lesson that relatability is not based on being right all the time, but in being real. The moment I peel back the layers and reveal my flaws is the moment people will begin to relate to me honestly. They know I'm not perfect.

 Brené Brown said that the two most powerful words in the English language are *Me, Too.* People want to know they are not alone in their own struggles. Genuine empathy cannot be faked. So maybe the first step to becoming authentic and genuine is admitting that we might be a bit skewed in how we view others—primarily due to how we view ourselves.

In the small sample size of people I sit with, self-loathing is epidemic. I recently sat with a young teenager who was contemplating suicide. Her parents had discovered a suicide pact on her phone and contacted me. I met her in a quiet corner of a restaurant and asked her, "How do you see you?" Before she could answer, a song began to softly play over the restaurant's speakers. It was Justin Bieber singing *Love Yourself.*

Two days later, I was sitting with a minister from a local church who was in an emotionally dark place. I asked the same question—and the same song began to play again. The upshot of the song is sarcasm, but that one line still rings true—we need to love ourselves.

 Insecurity demands that I must defend my position to an absurd extreme. Anything less might be perceived as weakness. When I am secure in who I am, I'm able to relax and engage in honest dialogue, realizing that I am more than my political beliefs and other people have wisdom that will help me see more clearly.

 That's why this is an internal job. Being comfortable in my own skin allows me to build genuine rapport with those who are different. I want them to be comfortable, as well. I want to be a person with the capacity to be around difference without requiring that people conform to my expectations. For me, this process can take lots of time and soul searching.

 In *No Man Is an Island*—written by one of my heroes, the late Catholic mystic Thomas Merton—he said, "The beginning of love is to let those we love be perfectly themselves, and not to twist them to fit our own image. Otherwise, we love only the reflection of ourselves we find in them." When we allow others to be themselves, it becomes a key for connecting with the genuine in both ourselves and others. I have a tendency to more completely trust others when I sense that they are being genuine with me.

 The most engaging people I know are comfortable being who they are. They are aware of what they do well, where they struggle. They are confident without being arrogant, and because of that they can hear others without feeling threatened. These are the most effective people at healing the rifts in our society.

Who Do You Think You Are?

 We notice our insecurities when they force us to either withdraw or posture as we engage in environments where we feel uncomfortable. Once we journey down that road, it is easy to lose sight of who we really are. We end up playing a role for so long that we lose touch with what is genuinely inside of us. I find it sad when people feel the need to pretend to be someone they are not, simply to be liked. One of the ways I help others turn that around is to share stories about myself that make me more fallible and human. I find when I'm vulnerable, others begin to relax.

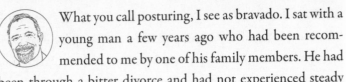

What you call posturing, I see as bravado. I sat with a young man a few years ago who had been recommended to me by one of his family members. He had been through a bitter divorce and had not experienced steady employment for more than a year, even though he was caring for three young children. I usually begin conversations with someone new by saying, "Tell me your story. Start at the beginning and don't leave anything out." It nearly always disarms the other person and makes them laugh a bit. It also communicates that I'm there to actually listen to them.

This young father was in so much pain over identity that he responded with how many Instagram followers he had. His intent was to impress rather than be genuine. Unfortunately, as I gently led him away from that and helped him take a look inside, he became agitated and angry. Finally, he stood up in the middle of the restaurant and announced that he was not about to be treated with disrespect. He had lost his sense of identity, preferring to talk about how many followers he had on social media.

One core component of being a peacemaker is the desire and ability to learn new things about yourself and others. Instead of being entrenched in our own personal dogma or singular experience, we can develop the ability to change and adapt. When we admit there are things we don't know, that vulnerability and humility will serve us well. It will allow us to show our strengths *and* weaknesses. The ability to admit wrong beliefs or assumptions is pivotal.

When I first met you, Arnita, I was surprised by how you so easily jumped into the conversation when some racially insensitive comments were made. You weren't offended, which would have been completely understandable. Instead, you began to playfully shoot what you later called "rubber bullets." Rather than lash out in offense and anger, you saw an opportunity to inform and educate. You didn't have to be so gracious, but you chose to change the narrative. From what I witnessed your choice was much more effective than offense would have been. It showed me how comfortable you are in your own skin. It was stunning, and it helped move the conversation forward.

I'm not sure that I'm always the most vulnerable person in the room, but I can assure you, I'm usually as real as it gets. I love that you called me playful. I'll never forget 2002, when my husband and I moved our little family from Atlanta to Dallas. We were driving a fair distance to Arlington to attend a traditional black church. One Wednesday evening, we decided to stick closer to home and attend a traditionally white church near our neighborhood.

The pastor preached a phenomenal message, but afterward, he looked in our direction and said, "It's wonderful to have the black family with us tonight." The four of us were the only African-Americans in the audience, so my face must have shown a bit of surprise at his statement. He realized what he had said and turned bright red with embarrassment. As it turns out, sitting right behind us was a family who had just returned from vacation whose last name was Black. At that point, what can you do except laugh? Laugh we did, for a while!

We've all experienced those moments when something was innocently said or done that could be construed by some as offensive. Most often, those in the room shift in their seats uncomfortably as they wait for the moment to pass. You didn't do that, Arnita. You laughed! And that laughter set others free from an awkward moment. Everyone has a tendency to say or do things that produce unintended results. You were comfortable enough in who you are to simply defuse the situation.

 Haven't we all had awkward moments over skin color or gender, or anything else where people draw lines of offense? I like to remind myself that I'm rarely the smartest person in the room. But, like your comment about being real, Arnita, I know that there aren't too many people who are more naturally curious than me. So, I'm comfortable enough to be curious. As a younger man, I would allow my insecurities to keep me sidelined. It's that age-old question: "Who do you think you are?" I always took that in a negative way, but these days, I ask myself that question often. "Who do I think I am?"

 Curiosity is the key to understanding and appreciating diversity. I'm a big believer in identifying those things that are important to you—your core values. One core value for me is diversity. Intentionally, I make a mental place to understand those whose experiences differ from mine— whether it be a different childhood or skin color. I always move toward diversity, not away from it.

 The fear of rejection can crush our curiosity. Inside, you may be curious and want to learn, but the fear that others might think less of you keeps you quiet. Often, after concluding a conversation, I'll ask myself—was I able to be me during that conversation? If not, I ask myself why. What prevented me from being open, relaxed, and honest? Whatever it is, it is also keeping me from growing.

•

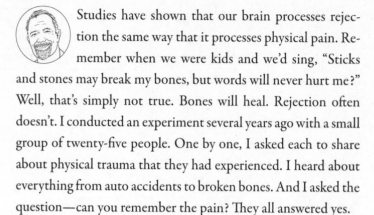

Studies have shown that our brain processes rejection the same way that it processes physical pain. Remember when we were kids and we'd sing, "Sticks and stones may break my bones, but words will never hurt me?" Well, that's simply not true. Bones will heal. Rejection often doesn't. I conducted an experiment several years ago with a small group of twenty-five people. One by one, I asked each to share about physical trauma that they had experienced. I heard about everything from auto accidents to broken bones. And I asked the question—can you remember the pain? They all answered yes.

Then I asked them to recall a time when they felt excluded or rejected. I heard stories filled with pain. And then something strange occurred. Nearly everyone in the room began to weep. When I asked which pain felt more real, they all said it was the pain of rejection. Studies have shown that our bodies actually store away the pain caused by rejection. It's always there, like instant recall, as if it just happened. It takes intentional effort on our part to move beyond that pain, but it's imperative.

Of course, the goal is to not give rejection a place to land, but I understand that is easier said than done, especially when we are young. It's possible, however, to work on our internal foundation so that we're secure enough not to take on someone else's rejection. For me, that comes from my faith in Jesus.

Recently my macho husband, Mike, took us for a pedicure. In the salon, two Korean ladies came to help us. They were talking to each other in Korean, laughing with each other while I was adjusting my massage chair. Suddenly Mike was stifling a laugh, so I asked him why he was laughing.

My husband was in the U.S. Army and was stationed in Korea

where he worked for a four-star general. He just so happens to understand the Korean language. He told me what one of them had said: "Good luck. He has some big-ass feet." I exploded in laughter as the ladies recoiled in humiliation.

We could have easily been angry and stormed out of the room, but they weren't lying. His feet are huge, and I love that my husband was secure enough to laugh it off rather than take offense.

Being unoffendable does not come naturally, but it is a gift to those around you. To help you learn this, spend most of your time with people who encourage you. It is helpful to build relational alliances with people you perceive as comfortable in their own skin. Take an inventory of your social circles. Insecurity begets insecurity; birds of a feather still flock together! Recognize where people promote or hinder your quest for security.

 As the old saying goes, it's important to find people who celebrate you rather than tolerate you.

 Years ago, I was invited to speak with a small leadership team from a church at a retreat. I was specifically asked to speak on the topic of grace, but on the second day, I realized that they weren't grasping it. I finally stopped and asked them, "Are you getting what I'm saying here?" A man in the group spoke up and perfectly summarized what I had been speaking on but did so with a bit of hostility. "Oh my goodness, you have got it!" I said with a hint of irony.

Then he responded, "If you think I'm going to let you get away with that, you're a bigger fool than I thought." I asked the others if he spoke for them too. I could tell that he didn't, but no one wanted to cross him, so they all nodded their heads in the affirmative.

I looked at the pastor and asked why he had even invited me. He replied, "I told you we don't have an understanding of grace." It seemed like I had only two options at that point. The first was I could talk about something else, or, secondly, we could agree I was the wrong speaker and I'd go home. The same man spoke up again and said, "You should go home." Again, I made sure it's what the others wanted, and no one disagreed. I wished them well, prayed for the rest of their day, went to my room, and packed up to leave. No one made a move to keep me there and I didn't even get paid for the weekend.

As I drove away, however, I found myself laughing at the sheer lunacy of the situation. I had been soundly rejected and to my complete surprise, I wasn't hurt. Later, I found out that others were deeply touched by how I handled that situation, but in that moment, I was aware that my acceptability didn't rest on the judgments of others. It's a great freedom and one that will serve you well in seeking to help others.

●

Try This

Crawl: *Think of a time when someone could have easily taken offense to a careless comment and chose not to. What did they say or do to disarm the situation?*

Walk: *What situations make you insecure? How can you effectively mitigate those feelings?*

Run: *Identify a person you perceive as being very comfortable in their own skin and connect with them in the next thirty days.*

7

Cultivating Compassion

────────────────●────────────────

Father Gregory Boyle, the author of the best-selling book Tattoos on
the Heart, once said "Here is what we seek: a compassion that can
stand in awe at what the poor have to carry rather than stand in
judgment at how they carry it."

Even though his focus was the poor, it's easy to insert the word
humanity into his thought. Compassion, although technically a
noun, is at its core, an action word. Being moved without taking ac-
tion is simply pity. Compassion will not allow us to feel and not act
on behalf of others.

I am convinced that life's mission is to teach us compassion. If so, why is it in such short supply? You
don't have to look far to see the selfish actions of
those seeking power, money, or both and how they remain obliv-
ious to those in need around them.

There are many reasons, of course, but the one I'm most concerned about is willful ignorance. When we consciously decide
not to know about someone, it makes it easier to disregard them
and the circumstances they face. If this indifference is the opposite of compassion, the antidote is willful understanding or
knowledge. It's hard to be indifferent to someone you know.

When I encounter a person who is homeless and asking for money, I don't worry how they'll spend the money. I know many who will only give food or something else they deem to be in the person's best interest. I don't see it that way. It's not my job to sit in judgment of whatever gets that person through the day, whether it be a Big Mac or a beer.

It is clear that compassion requires empathy for divergent points of view. I was once asked to be on the board of a crisis pregnancy center. They literally told me I'd be perfect for their set of criteria, which included having a minority presence. Compassion, for me, demands that we comfort and support all women regardless of their choice. Love isn't selective based on my judgments.

That mind-set cuts across religious and political lines. Compassion is a genuine concern for the sufferings and misfortunes of others. There are usually no winners with abortion. Those who have them are suffering. Those who don't are, as well.

Judging others will always keep compassion at bay. As I've allowed myself to fall in love with humanity, I've become aware that I can no longer be judge and jury. Instead I have stepped off the bench and stand alongside the "defendants" as their friend.

A Life of Intentional Compassion

I was once invited to a financial planning meeting with some who could best be described as high rollers. The question was asked, "Do you have any conflict enjoying the money you have in a world with so much need around you?" As I looked around, I was surprised to see so many facial expressions that seemed confused by the question. Obviously, they didn't, and said so. I do. Every day.

When the speaker went on to ask why not, most responded that they had worked hard for what they had and never thought twice about enjoying a larger slice of the world's pie. The unspoken inference, of course, is that poor people don't work as hard, so they are only getting what they deserve. It's only one of the lies wealthy people tell themselves so they can ignore the needs of others as they plunge headlong into their own amusement. Every time I drive past a strawberry field in my county and watch the farm workers bent over picking strawberries, I know I don't work that hard. I haven't since I got off my dad's farm.

You can remain callous only if you don't actually know people who have very little, who work hard for what they do have and have few other options to move beyond it. And I don't mean just knowing *about* them, but actually knowing *them* individually. When you do, your compassion will grow.

 Barry Switzer, the former football coach, said many people were born on third base, but think they hit a triple. I didn't choose to be born a white male in America any more than an orphan in Mozambique chose their life. If we look differently, we'll find compassion is more of a telescope than a microscope. It's a wider lens, helping us see what's beyond our own experience, and not just see them, but empathize and engage.

Intentionality is key. Especially as we place ourselves in unfamiliar situations with others who are not like us. When I was in business, I was often required to attend mixers and dinners with politicians, leaders, and other business people. Every single time, I was the guy in the corner—afraid to even initiate a conversation. When I was in sales, I would die a bit on the inside every time I had to make a cold call. However, I intentionally stepped through those fears time and again and, eventually, they disappeared completely.

My wife, Danette, was my coach during those years. Even though she's an introvert by nature, she naturally exudes compassion. She literally would force me to stop and engage the hurting, broken, and homeless. Absent that part of my journey, I would never have stepped in to care for the poorest children in my city—those who live in hotels and trailers on Union Avenue. For the past nine years I have put on a Santa suit and passed out toys to the least of these. Without question it's the highlight of my year.

There's a great book by Eugene H. Peterson called *A Long Obedience in the Same Direction*. There's power in changing our course with intent and purpose.

 A few years ago, I was approached about doing some teaching in Kenya. In all honesty, I didn't want to. I don't run a mission organization and there was nothing in me that desired to get involved in the lives of people in Africa. I can barely keep up with the need here. Over time, I couldn't ignore their persistent requests, however, and I agreed to go down the road simply to see where it led.

I walked the land where tribal violence killed thousands of people after a disputed election in 2008. I was overwhelmed, not only by the need there, but also with compassion for those living through it. I discovered how insulated my world was. Seeing fellow humans suffer changes you and opens your heart to discover how you can help.

Often times, we don't want to know about the single mom with two kids who is barely surviving, or the injustice in Syria. As for those starving in Kenya, we eventually partnered with those whose hearts were broken for the children of their region. A few years later they discovered another group of 100,000 no-madic people in Pokot who were starving in a five-year drought that killed their cattle. No government aid or non-governmental organization (NGO) was there. So, the Kenyans we knew—who live with very little—asked us if we could help others who had even less. They have generously given their time and we have sent them more than two million dollars from people who listen to my podcast. We have given them food and water, and we are now helping them build a sustainable post-nomadic life.

Here's the lesson: We simply moved our feet in a direction that seemed right. The journey did not begin with compassion, but that's definitely where it thrives now.

Building Bridges to Others

Author J. K. Rowling said, "Indifference and neglect often do much more damage than outright dislike." Indifference is a huge roadblock to compassion, and learning compassion is a journey. I step into relationships intentionally; I don't wait for them to come to me. Compassion blossoms as I get to know people and their experiences.

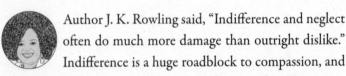

My son-in-law, Josh, recently moved his T-shirt screen printing business from his home, where he's been for twelve years, to an industrial space. Soon after, two men walked in to order custom shirts for their wedding. Similar to the bakers who don't want to decorate cakes for same-sex weddings, he had to make a decision. Two men getting married is outside of his experience and, likely, his comfort zone. I was proud of him, though, as he asked all the right questions: What would you like the shirts to say? How many do you need?

When do you need them?

As he told me, "They're human beings and it's a T-shirt." I was a proud father-in-law, because that's the perfect example that agreement is not always necessary to practice compassion.

 There's something wonderful about stepping outside of our own story to engage others with empathy and understanding. Canadian philosopher Jean Vanier said in *Called to Community*, "Welcoming is not just something that happens as people cross the threshold. It is an attitude; it is the constant openness of the heart; it is saying to people every morning and at every moment 'come in'; it is giving them space; it is listening to them attentively. To welcome means listening a great deal to people and then discerning the truth with them."

 Having compassion doesn't always require a passport or a trip to another country. I believe compassion is awakened by suffering even if we don't suffer at the hands of the same thing. Opportunities exist all around us, whether that be bringing in your neighbor's trash can or buying coffee for the car behind you in line at McDonald's.

A few years ago, IHOP was celebrating their sixtieth anniversary by offering a short stack of pancakes for just sixty cents. Even though I don't have a deep, abiding love for pancakes, I knew someone who did. So I invited them out to breakfast. While there, we noticed a young mother with a two-year-old child. They were soon joined by a much older woman. They all ordered pancakes, which totaled $1.80. I didn't know their story, but I was moved for them. I discreetly asked the waitress if they had ordered anything beyond the pancakes. They had ordered a single pork chop. As I left, I paid for their meal. I wrote a note on the paid receipt telling them how beautiful their family was. We have opportunities every day to practice compassion with those already around us.

We can also be intentional about that proximity, can't we?

Arnita, years ago you moved from a black community in the south to a mostly white suburb in North Texas. What you discovered can't be taught in a class or read in a book.

Wayne, you jumped on a plane bound for Kenya to explore a story firsthand. You had to go and see for yourself.

Proximity is definitely important, but in all three of our stories, we created our own. In each instance, we needed courage to move forward into a new level of understanding. Courage is simply doing something that scares you. When you combine courage with compassion, the world can change.

Compassion Makes You Better

I love how compassion changed me. There are many positive effects of living a life filled with compassion. Studies suggest that compassion helps us recover faster from sickness and disease, and it also lengthens our lives. It makes sense to me. I feel better when I help others. Compassion is often a cure for loneliness because it shifts our focus off ourselves onto others.

Medical Science Monitor published an article in 2011 linking the neurobiological effects of compassion and love. They found that those who regularly practice compassion often experience new pathways in their brains—pathways that lead to a deeper capacity for love. This is the ultimate win-win. A compassionate outlook also redirects our sense of awareness.

When I walk into any place filled with people, whether it be a grocery store, Starbucks, or church, I'm scanning the space in a different manner than most. I was a frequent patron of a restaurant that doubled as my counseling office. I met people there nearly every weekday for food and conversation. One particular day, I was walking to my car after meeting someone when an older, homeless woman, who also happened to be deaf, approached me. I had encountered her before and did my best to encourage her through prayer, conversation, and food, but this day was different.

I had hosted a video show earlier in the day, so instead of my normal wardrobe of shorts and a T-shirt, I was fully dressed in slacks and a sport coat. As she approached, she smiled. "You look nice today," she said, in her best voice and sign language. We talked for a while before I got in my car. Once inside, I began to weep at what had just taken place. I began to thank God aloud for the gift of being known by the forgotten and marginalized. To this day, it's one of the best gifts I've ever received.

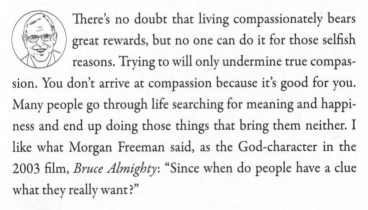 There's no doubt that living compassionately bears great rewards, but no one can do it for those selfish reasons. Trying to will only undermine true compassion. You don't arrive at compassion because it's good for you. Many people go through life searching for meaning and happiness and end up doing those things that bring them neither. I like what Morgan Freeman said, as the God-character in the 2003 film, *Bruce Almighty*: "Since when do people have a clue what they really want?"

 Honestly, I may not be the easiest choice as someone's first African-American female friend, but I'm always glad it's me. These relationships create such a ripe environment to learn from each other in ways that cannot be manufactured or planned. We learn how to challenge our opinions, to care at a deeper level, to show empathy, and to understand sensitivity around each other's varied priorities.

One of my favorite quotes comes from Bill Bullard: "Opinion is the lowest form of human knowledge. It requires no accountability, no understanding. The highest form of knowledge is empathy, for it requires us to suspend our egos and live in another's world. It requires profound purpose larger than the self-kind of understanding."

Three Levels of Compassion

 Compassion is a primary tool of a peacemaker. I see multiple levels of compassion—primary, secondary, and tertiary. Each level is related to conduct and different degrees of connectivity. Primary compassion occurs with people we directly know and share proximity. Of course, primary compassion is the most personal and passionate level. Secondary compassion refers to a person attached to someone I know. Tertiary compassion is practiced when we connect with organizations that are near and dear to those people we know. When compassion is defined this way, it can be viewed as concentric circles providing lots of options for us to practice.

 Sometimes tertiary compassion doesn't work. I was recently in a meeting with the chief of police discussing the homeless in my affluent town in Southern California. The average household income here is above the national average, so someone suggested simply tapping into the wealthy residents who had generous hearts. It made perfect sense. We could build a center and provide support for the 3,500 homeless in our area. But the Chief told us that once word got out that we had built such a center, 55,000 homeless from around Southern California would invade the community. We can't do it here until other communities do it, as well. A systemic solution wasn't possible for one community alone. Sometimes the best solutions are personal rather than systemic.

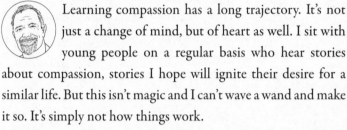 Learning compassion has a long trajectory. It's not just a change of mind, but of heart as well. I sit with young people on a regular basis who hear stories about compassion, stories I hope will ignite their desire for a similar life. But this isn't magic and I can't wave a wand and make it so. It's simply not how things work.

Life is equal parts journey and process. Many of my experiences are the fruit of a heart that has been broken, often against its will. We have chased more dreams than I can remember, but never with what most would call success. I've experienced the pain of a daughter who was molested for two years right under my nose at a mainstream, denominational church.

For me, the pain in the journey was well on its way to producing anger, resentment, and bitterness. At that point, I could have become the guy standing on the porch yelling at the neighborhood kids, "Get off my lawn, you hooligans!" Except I probably wouldn't say hooligans.

Instead, I began to view life and people through a different lens, noticing those who were a bit bruised, just like me. True empathy of that magnitude became my road map to compassion.

When you get close to people, you'll find they are just like you. That's where compassion can take root.

•

Try This

Crawl: *Learn to listen with compassion without invalidating the other person's position or feelings. Take note of how often you use words like always or never in talking about others. See if you can eliminate those words in such discourse.*

Walk: *In the next three days, look for one way to show a random act of compassion to another person. How does it make you feel about yourself?*

Run: *Model compassion by scheduling time with someone you can bless.*

8

Listen Up!

━━━━━━━━━━━━━━━━━━━━━━━━●━━━━━━━━━━━━━━━━━━━━━━━━

The Urban Dictionary defines listen up as something you say to people who have no idea what's going on. How often do we react to people around us without an understanding or appreciation for what is happening in their life?

Everyone has a story. Some tell it eagerly. Some need it drawn out. But for many the pathway to healing begins with someone willing to listen to their story. Several years ago, I was part of a local outreach to the homeless population. We would hand out chicken sandwiches to people on the street. I was surprised that so many people wanted to tell me how they ended up homeless. Many of them had made one bad decision that landed them on the streets—one moment with far-reaching consequences.

In our previous chapter, we focused on compassion. Listening to others—to hear and to acknowledge someone's story—is a critical component that will help express and grow our compassion. If you interpret someone else's words in your own framework, you have no idea what they are trying to say. You have to interpret it in theirs. Learning any language involves hearing as much as speaking. The good news is that listening is a skill we can all develop to make us more effective communicators and healers.

I knew the gender of both of my children before they were born. I named them both in utero and communicated with them daily. After my youngest son was born by Cesarean section, the nurses laid him on a table beside me. When I spoke his name, "Nolan," he turned his head toward me. The nurse was amazed. She said, "You must have talked to him during your pregnancy."

Of course I did. My newborn was already learning language by hearing language. My oldest son would always hear me call my husband "Mike" and started to do so as well, which reinforces just how much of our language comes from what we hear.

As we further delve into speaking the language of healing, one imperative practice is the importance of listening to others. Sometimes, the language of healing will be verbal in nature based on what you say or how you respond. Other times, the language of healing will be nonverbal based on the depth of your listening.

Years ago, I was a general manager for a large lumber company in Southern California. One of the most valuable things they taught me was to put down my pen—or whatever I had in my hand—or to step away from the computer when talking with someone. The simple act of making eye contact let the person know that I was paying attention and valued them.

Prior to that, I would typically respond in a disinterested manner, "Yeah, go ahead. What do you need?" And typically, I continued working at my desk without even looking up at them. The moment I began to put the pen down, the morale of the team increased dramatically. Attentive listening communicates that the person in front of you is not an imposition, but someone of value.

Building Rapport

Good listening puts us in the moment. Because of our constant media access, most people argue politics with someone like Sean Hannity or Rachel Maddow when neither of them is even in the room. In doing so, they get caught up in stereotypes designed to fuel debate and increase ratings, rather than encourage dialogue.

When I mediate conflicts, I observe that pattern often. As soon as someone starts talking, others in the room find a box to put them in, be it liberal, conservative, or some other designation. I can visually observe them preparing their rebuttal without listening to what that person is actually saying. Most of the time when they respond, they talk like a pundit on cable news.

We really don't know what people think until we hear them out. When we do, we realize how flawed our judgments are. If we can be touched by someone else's story, we can begin to build rapport that will help us work together.

Listening is foundational to any good relationship. It brings you closer and provides presence, which allows real conversations to bubble up. Active listening is hard. It has both a physical and an emotional component to it because it involves both hearing and comprehending simultaneously. It is particularly hard for me because as a scientist I am solution driven. Shutting that off helps me listen.

We can all look for ways to become effective listeners. People who speak the language of healing will be able to listen to others even if they hold nothing in common with them. That's the key to becoming a master at listening. Your attentive ear gives them value and significance. It promotes healing in our culture.

Rapport builds trust and helps us avoid socially awkward situations and inaccurate assumptions. We all view others through lenses we may not even be aware of. As I said before, I was raised in a rural area of Oregon by a stepfather whose views were filtered through generational racism. It was simply how he was taught, but his view of the world colored my perceptions. I've spent my entire adult life relearning. Well, maybe a better word would be unlearning. When I sit with people, I have to consciously pull off those lenses. If not, I'll inevitably jump to conclusions based on the way I was raised. Filters can be powerful, and the ones I was given have no place in someone else's personal narrative.

When I listen well, I often find myself surprised by the uniqueness and individuality of others. But that's only when I'm actively listening—when I remove my lenses or presuppositions about others. Any preconceived notions I have about someone, whether they are gay, Muslim, or millennial, does not serve either of us well.

After years of being someone who would pretend to have all the answers, I had an epiphany—I don't know everything. As soon as I became comfortable enough to say, "I don't know," it allowed others to relax and actually trust me at a deeper level. As a result, I'm a better listener than I am an advice-giver, although many people might say I give decent advice. My main task on this earth is to sit with people, connect with them, and let them be known by me. As I've lived a fair portion of my life, I've come to believe that the universal cry of humanity is simply to be seen and told they're okay.

I don't think there's a person on this earth who I can't sit with for two minutes and not find something in common. I was just listening to a podcast with Lara Logan, a journalist for *60*

Minutes who has worked in the world's most critical hot spots. "We all love our children. We all want the best. It doesn't matter. Even terrorists love their children." This reality invites me to drill right in with others to relate and find common desires and experiences.

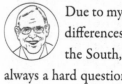 Due to my frequent travel, people often ask me what differences I notice between people in the Northeast, the South, or even in Africa, Europe, or Asia. That's always a hard question for me. I'm far more engaged by what I hold in common with people around the world. I'm not blind to the differences I can see in our cultures, languages, experiences, or dress. During most of my travels, I stay in people's homes, not hotels, and sometimes those homes are in impoverished neighborhoods.

In spite of those differences, I'm amazed at our similarities. When I hear someone's struggles, empathy is never far away. That hasn't always been the case. The first person I traveled with overseas helped me see how I conveyed an air of superiority to people who didn't do things the same way we did in the States. That distanced me from the people I'd come to visit.

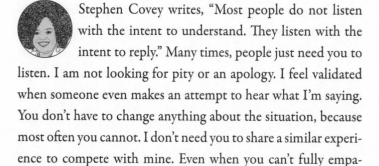 Stephen Covey writes, "Most people do not listen with the intent to understand. They listen with the intent to reply." Many times, people just need you to listen. I am not looking for pity or an apology. I feel validated when someone even makes an attempt to hear what I'm saying. You don't have to change anything about the situation, because most often you cannot. I don't need you to share a similar experience to compete with mine. Even when you can't fully empathize, you can still listen well.

Listening can reduce animosity and anger. We don't all have

the same experiences, and we don't need to pretend we do. Let's have conversations over equity, injustice, compassion, and difference anyway! No downplaying. No minimizing. No demonizing one another. No victim-shaming.

 I met with a couple who have tragically lost two adult children in their life—one to leukemia and the other to a traffic accident. I've never lost a child, so I can't sit with them and pretend to understand their pain. But I can do my best to see life through their eyes.

Not wanting their children to be erased, they have a desire to talk about them. Most of their friends, however, fear that dialogue will only create more pain and thus avoid it. I can only imagine what it must feel like to lose one child, much less two. I'm sure the pain is a hundred times worse than anything I can imagine. Listening helps us evade the hollow words of false comfort.

A Soft Place to Land

 As humans, we tend to run from suffering. It's simply easier to focus on happy things. After 9/11, a friend of mine talked about the meaning of compassion. It literally means to come to "passion." In the Old English sense of the word, passion means to suffer. While victims were running out of the World Trade Center, the first responders were literally running into it. That's compassion, to run to the sufferings of others. It's the desire to help others, without shielding ourselves from the risk or the possibility of pain.

As a teenager, I worked at an airport to earn flight training. I noticed that every time an airplane crashed in that part of California, everyone there would suspect pilot-error even before they knew the cause. It wasn't because they had innate suspicions of other pilots, but because they were trying to mask their own feelings of vulnerability. When you fly a small plane, you want to believe that if you do everything right it won't crash. No one wants to believe that something catastrophic could happen that a competent pilot couldn't overcome. So they turn on one another as a form of self-protection. That's what many do with pain. They don't want to contemplate theirs, so they don't want to talk about yours.

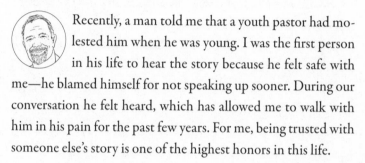

Recently, a man told me that a youth pastor had molested him when he was young. I was the first person in his life to hear the story because he felt safe with me—he blamed himself for not speaking up sooner. During our conversation he felt heard, which has allowed me to walk with him in his pain for the past few years. For me, being trusted with someone else's story is one of the highest honors in this life.

If we're going to be in those conversations, we have to be a soft place for others to land. People will only open up like that when they suspect we can be trusted with their story while being safe with their heart. That's why people who are judgmental, uncaring, or not discreet will not be invited into the depth of human pain. And it's a good thing they are not.

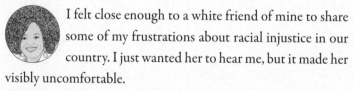

I felt close enough to a white friend of mine to share some of my frustrations about racial injustice in our country. I just wanted her to hear me, but it made her visibly uncomfortable.

I knew she was not a safe place to land and her desire to not listen limited the scope and depth of our friendship. Her response surprised and saddened me. If I thought that she wasn't able to engage I would never have gone to her. I'd known her for many years and thought she would care, because I cared. Think about it. If a close friend was uncomfortable listening to my concern, even if she didn't share it, it's no wonder people who don't know each other well find it nearly impossible to have a meaningful conversation.

A Christian music artist, Lecrae, wrote a song about his experiences along those lines. To that point, his music and message had been fully accepted as he headlined concerts around the world. There came a day, however, when he realized that the white church viewed justice through a completely different lens.

They blankly stared when he mentioned Trayvon Martin and they were sure Michael Brown must have done something wrong. He was stunned that they didn't share his concern for what he saw as obvious and systemic injustice. After years of feeling he was just banging his head against a wall, he made the hard choice to exit the relationship and wrote an article about divorcing the white church.

Learning to Listen Well

Since we have established that listening builds rapport, increases opportunities for discovery and learning, and challenges our levels of understanding and humility, what are some ways to practice listening and understanding without judging or profiling?

I find it helpful to suspend my personal agenda in conversations like this. If we come to a conversation with an agenda for a specific outcome, the tendency is to twist everything to achieve our desired outcome. These days, my agenda is to simply listen to the concerns others have and see if we can find a gracious way to work toward a solution together.

If I need to convince you of anything, our ability to work together diminishes. When we sense we are being used, we have a tendency to shut down. I might nod in the affirmative or say words of agreement, but as soon as I walk out of the room, it's over. That's not a conversation, that's coercion. Great listening allows us to be in a conversation without knowing the outcome.

I will often begin a discussion with, "The first thing you should know about me is that I'm not you. A lot more will make sense after that." I read that quote once and loved it! I apply that to people I listen to so I don't make assumptions about how to interpret their words. I ask a lot of questions to make sure I'm really hearing them.

Intentionally harnessing our personal filters is the key to active listening without making judgments. We can't help but be shaped by our experiences. I tend to control or manage my filters by forcing objectivity into the act of listening. I think *who, what, when, why, how,* and *where* so my emotions work for the positive. Instead of being self-centric, force your thoughts to be others-centric.

Turning my filters off takes an act of will. I have to be very intentional. Every day I ask God to give me the lenses of heaven, allowing me to see the way that he sees rather than the way that I'm prone to see. I practiced this daily until it became reality for me. Every morning, I would consciously remove the lenses of experience and replace them with fresh ones. It probably took a year to become second nature, but it did. I rarely enter a room with preconceived notions anymore, at least as best I know. The Book of Lamentations says, "His mercies are new every morning." If that's the truth, then the least I can do is give every new day—and every person I encounter—a fresh start.

This quote by Margaret Wheatley sums it up for me: *"Listening is such a simple act. It requires us to be present, and that takes practice, but we don't have to do anything else. We don't have to advise, or coach, or sound wise. We just have to be willing to sit there and listen. If we can do that, we create moments in which real healing is available. Whatever life we have experienced, if we can tell our story to someone who listens, we find it easier to deal with our circumstances."*

Try This

Crawl: *Listen to someone this week to understand them; not to solve their problem or rebut their conclusion. It is rarely necessary to add your thoughts to their story unless invited to do so. If you need more clarity, use these phrases:*

- *"Help me understand..."*
- *"Please explain..."*
- *"What's your experience with..."*
- *"What are your thoughts on..."*

Walk: *After conversations, journal why or why not you may have found it difficult to listen and understand what the person was trying to communicate.*

Run: *Practice. Practice. Practice.*

9

From My Good to Our Good

———————————◉———————————

It's often not that hard to know what I think is good for me. We know our own needs well and have a sense of fairness built around our preferences. However, looking beyond my individual good to see what is best for others around me is something else altogether. Moving from my good, to all of our good, is a great test of maturity.

Individualism is a powerful reality when it challenges us to take care of ourselves and rise to whatever life our talents and diligence can take us. But when it means everyone grabs for their own, without regard to what is fair for all, it can be incredibly destructive.

What creates an environment that allows someone to shift from looking out for their own interests, to embracing a common good that ensures the same opportunities, protections, and freedoms for others that I want for myself?

One of the early words you hear from any child is "mine," especially when toys are involved. A good parent helps their child see beyond that self-centric world to include siblings early on, and then friends and class-mates. We hope to break that in our children and our grandchildren, but it rarely lasts into adulthood.

We usually do that through punishment. So, if children share only fearing something worse, it's still egocentric, right?

When I've helped people negotiate common ground agreements, we begin with most people in the room fighting for their good at the expense of someone else's. Unfortunately, politics is always weighted advantageously for the powerful who force their will on others, rather than negotiating the mythical level playing field most people say they want.

But a marvelous moment happens when people in that room begin to think beyond what is good for them, to what is also good for those from whom they differ.

We Belong to Each Other

 We live in an individualistic society. We do not easily think as a collective society. Perhaps earlier in human development, we understood the value of collectivism, but now in America it seems not a priority. I don't know where the switch flips from me to we, recognizing that we are interconnected.

Mother Teresa said, "We lose our peace when we forget we belong to each other."

 Wasn't that the idea behind our civics education in school? *E pluribus unum*. Everything we do affects others. That is a steep learning curve, however, since it is so natural to look out for our own interests. That's especially true of those who are part of the dominant culture. They have access to the conventions of society, so they think everyone can get what they want if they work hard enough. That myth actually keeps us from caring about true justice and fairness for others and growing into a selflessness that includes others. That's why those who are marginalized usually have greater hope for collective responsibility and care.

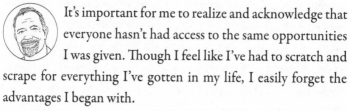 It's important for me to realize and acknowledge that everyone hasn't had access to the same opportunities I was given. Though I feel like I've had to scratch and scrape for everything I've gotten in my life, I easily forget the advantages I began with.

Even the good we do for others can have a selfish motive. Whether it's curbing the AIDS epidemic in Africa or giving to a charity, there are often accolades to make us feel good in the end. Is anything truly selfless?

 I do think selflessness is possible. It is a heart condition. I know there are people who intentionally act sacrificially to benefit others rather than themselves.

 True enough, there are many people in my life who I would step in front of a bus for, like my children, grandchildren, and close friends. That would be selfless in that there is no reward for me. I would put myself right in the path without giving it a second thought, but that's for people I know well.

 Selflessness commences as a thought and then requires action. Many live at such a fast pace they don't see the needs of others right in front of them.

Last year, I was in a local resale shop when I noticed a woman and her young daughter trying to get a bookcase into their van. I watched them struggle for about five minutes then I went up to them and offered to transfer it in my SUV. Of course, initially, the lady was hesitant and even startled. I assured her I would not steal it and that I would follow her six miles to her home.

A few weeks later, I saw her again. She greeted me by my name! I was so surprised because I did not remember hers. She told me that she prays for me every day when she sees the bookcase in her classroom. Although her heartfelt prayers were a bonus, my act to help her had no strings attached. Those who speak the language of healing will help and advocate for total strangers.

 We hear many stories of people doing heroic things for others they don't even know, like pulling people from a burning car or jumping into a rushing river to save a stranger being swept away.

Tapping the Passion for Fairness

 One of the things I've tapped into in helping people find common ground is a personal sense of fairness. Fairness always polls well. It only takes one person in a room to start talking about fairness and it taps something deep in the human spirit; even people who come for very selfish reasons will see how compelling that is. Most people want fairness because they feel at some point in their lives they were treated unfairly.

Anecdotally, I would say 75 to 80 percent are motivated by fairness to seek a collective good. When they find your cash-filled wallet in a parking lot they are going to turn it in. The other 20 percent will keep it, willing to use whatever advantage comes their way, even if it cheats others. Unfortunately, many of our lobbyists seem to come from that 20 percent, as do many of our politicians. They write laws that give one side an advantage over the other, one company gets benefits others don't. If they were custodians of a common good, they'd be tapping into that sense of fairness. They wouldn't just think what's best for my client, my party, or my career, but what is fair for all Americans. That's where you'll find true statesmen and stateswomen.

I was in a court proceeding with lawyers and judges where no one cared about what was true. I was encouraged to lie to my advantage to match the duplicity of the other party. The judge fed the plaintiff's attorney exactly what lie he needed to tell to keep the court case from being thrown out. I also know stories of prosecutors offering a plea to someone they knew was innocent, just before dropping the charges. If our justice system doesn't bend toward fairness, what hope have we?

There's enough fairness in the American spirit to tap, but we don't give people that opportunity. When I've done mediation, I told those inviting me that if I couldn't get to 80 percent agreement, they didn't have to pay me. That was our target and I always got paid. People came to the room fighting for what they wanted but when given the opportunity to fight for fairness, they did. They always did.

Jesus challenged his followers to treat one another the same way they wanted to be treated. One hundred and forty-three other religions have that same admonishment embedded in their ethics.

The Golden Rule in *The Message* translation of the Bible reads, "Ask yourself what you want people to do for you, then grab the initiative and do it for them." Mosaic law had a similar command, "Whatever is hurtful to you, do not do it to any other person."

In other words, if someone's action has hurt you, do not do that to someone else. The motivation is not wanting others to feel the hurt you have felt. A great deal of healing and compassion can result from this focus. It offers us a more selfless way to think.

 Doesn't it have a lot to do with the environment we live in? Most people want to share equally, but as soon as someone makes a move to the front of the buffet line, others move in quickly to stake out their spot in line. If we leave it open to human selfishness, we seem to follow the worst examples. Getting more people to think of others would provide far better ones.

Learning to Think Beyond Ourself

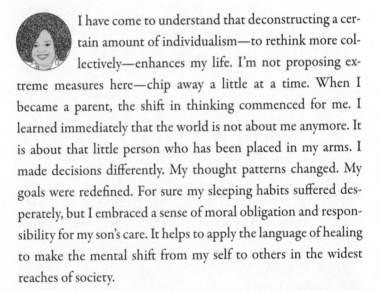 I have come to understand that deconstructing a certain amount of individualism—to rethink more collectively—enhances my life. I'm not proposing extreme measures here—chip away a little at a time. When I became a parent, the shift in thinking commenced for me. I learned immediately that the world is not about me anymore. It is about that little person who has been placed in my arms. I made decisions differently. My thought patterns changed. My goals were redefined. For sure my sleeping habits suffered desperately, but I embraced a sense of moral obligation and responsibility for my son's care. It helps to apply the language of healing to make the mental shift from my self to others in the widest reaches of society.

Parenting sure helped me get beyond myself. What values did I want to instill in my children? American author H. Jackson Brown said, "Live so that when your children think of fairness, caring, and integrity, they think of you."

I really love how parenting and grandparenting taught me

how to look outside of my own little world. I'm not just responsible for caring for my daughters. I need to feel that same caring for others, too.

I recently sat with a young woman who was trafficked for sex during a period of several years. She's twenty-two years old. She's beautiful and bright but got caught in a horrible situation. I tapped into it because I sat down, took a breath, and asked her to tell me her story. I had no idea that this was part of who she was. Now that I know her, I can't ignore her.

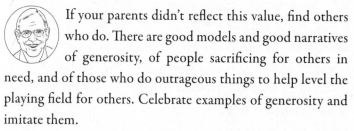 If your parents didn't reflect this value, find others who do. There are good models and good narratives of generosity, of people sacrificing for others in need, and of those who do outrageous things to help level the playing field for others. Celebrate examples of generosity and imitate them.

I'm afraid some of my conservative friends are going to see socialism here and react, but this is less about the government caring for everybody as it is for us to care about each other. If you've ever been marginalized, you know what it feels like and you wouldn't want anyone you care about to endure it.

However, most people already feel challenged by the demands of their own lives and it can be overwhelming to even consider the needs of those outside our existing relationships.

If me and mine have ours, we are less concerned for those who didn't get theirs.

Expanding into those wider reaches of society Arnita mentioned earlier takes an intentional choice. But we don't have to know every person who is unlike me—just a few, and compassion can extrapolate from there. The more people we care about, the more we'll seek the fairness that common good demands.

Cultural Intelligence

 I find David Livermore's description of cultural intelligence to be helpful here. I was introduced to his work while in graduate school. He posits four aspects of cultural intelligence: motivation or drive, gaining knowledge of other cultures, developing a strategy to involve yourself with those cultures, and taking action to engage them. If I go to China and I look someone directly in the eyes, it would convey a totally different message than it does in America.

Cultural intelligence awakens your consciousness to differences in how people live and act. It helps us not assume that everyone thinks like we do or follows the same customs. And it's best applied at the micro level, person to person, not just in the generalities of a culture.

 Although he assures me I may, when I am with my Muslim friend, I don't eat bacon. That's Respect 101, right? I know that if I started drinking alcohol around him and got just the least bit inebriated, his religion would tell him to leave. He's forbidden to even be around its effects, so I make the choice to proceed with respectful understanding.

 That's why the Golden Rule doesn't encourage us to do to others what I think is best for them, which is often condescending and rude. When I travel, I often stay in people's homes. Some of my hosts want to share with me everything that's meaningful and enjoyable for them. I don't mind that because I am their guest. Others write me in advance to find out my favorite foods, likes and dislikes, just like Arnita did when Bob and I first came to Dallas. You didn't want me visiting your home and eating your favorite foods but you wanted me to enjoy mine. That's real hospitality.

I've been in parts of the world where *hospitality* can be overwhelming. They burden me with expectations that serve their culture more than my comfort. Sometimes, it is oppressive. I deal with it because I am willing to take them however they are. When you're in my home, I want to know what you like and what makes you comfortable so you can be at home where I live.

As I apply cultural intelligence, deference is critical for me. Deference is yielding to the needs of others out of respect. Deference is others-focused. Deference respects difference. Deference plays an enormous role in being a peacemaker, who speaks the language of healing.

When you two first came to Dallas, I asked about your favorite foods. Although Wayne's favorite food is fried chicken, he didn't mention it because it could have been an offense since it's a negative stereotype about African-Americans. That's cultural intelligence.

Growing into a Larger World

The real shift in culture comes when people who hold the levers of power really become others-focused. In reality, white men too often dominate the power structure in the United States. Our country's original documents were probably written to your ancestors, white landowners. So, I'm curious: How did you two go from being self-focused to being others-focused and inviting others in? How did you combat social selection?

As a young man, I discovered an absolute love of basketball. People think of Bakersfield as a bit of a redneck place, but there is a pretty diverse cultural aspect to our city. When I began to play basketball five times a week, I often found myself in a minority context as the only white guy on the court.

I had to step in there and be part of the team. These men became my dear friends and still are. During that time Steve, who was a bit older than me, went to lunch with me. When I went to pay the bill, I pulled out my wallet. He saw my driver's license and he looked at me and said, "Wait a minute, your middle name is LeRoy? Oh, wait until everybody hears about this."

I begged him not to tell anyone! The next time I walked into the gym at Cal State Bakersfield, the coach of the team called out, "LeRoy!" I shook my head as he went on, "You got the name, but let's get one thing clear—you ain't got the game."

I grew up in a lily-white area of Oregon. Basketball was the gift that allowed me to encounter men of color and discover that none of us needed to be scared of the other. We're all just doing the best we can on the court trying to get one over on the other. If I had not experienced diversity through organized sports, I would never have asked Emad to go to breakfast. Sports taught me how to care about people who aren't like me.

I love how that happened relationally for you. It happened in a more principled way for me. As a young man, I was taught character and fairness. Though I grew up in a farming community that didn't have a lot of black people, it did have a lot of people of Mexican descent, both working in our vineyard and attending school with me. I didn't have a sense of their humanity being different, but I didn't have a sensitivity to what challenges they faced in the culture, either.

As I grew older, I developed a real passion for justice and fairness. Even though I'm a white male who has voted mostly Republican, I don't admire many of the white males who hold power in our society. I don't respect the CEOs that take a disproportionate amount of reward off the table at the expense of their workers. I'm not a socialist, but I'm driven by a sense of fairness—not just for me, but for all of us. I was inspired by Nelson Mandela's book, *Long Walk to Freedom*. I love that twenty-five years of hard labor in prison didn't make him bitter and wanting to punish those who oppressed him and his people. After all he suffered, he sought reconciliation not retribution.

When I got out of my high school, I went to a university where I met many people from different cultures and that expanded my heart. That's continued throughout adulthood: Recently I had the opportunity to help tribes of nomadic people in Africa who were dying from the impact of a prolonged drought. I had small grandchildren when we first heard about them and I could not look at my grandchildren and not see other faces around the world who didn't have enough to eat.

I recognize that I was born on third base. I'm not apologetic about it, but I know I didn't earn it. At the same time, I don't suffer from "white guilt" or try to put it on others. I come from a faith that says if you've been given much, then much will be required of you. Generosity touches my heart for good in the same way injustice disturbs my soul.

What a powerful conversation! Rarely do people like me hear that humble perspective from people like you. Studies show that diversity and sensitivity training in the workplace oftentimes backfire because this encouragement needs to come from the dominant culture.

Our conversations confirm how much we've come to learn

about one another, which reduces false assumptions. These are the kinds of conversations that facilitate healing and drive out conflict. We are well aware of the risk, courage, and tenderness necessary for this to happen, but are also aware that it is possible.

●

Try This

Crawl: *In conversations about different racial views, how do you inject denial, minimization, or victim-shaming into someone else's story and how do you feel it has been used against you? How can you avoid doing that in the future?*

Walk: *Examine how your racial views were shaped in your formative years. Summarize them and discuss with a friend how they affect you today.*

Run: *This week, intentionally defend someone different from you to someone who is like you.*

10

Willing to be Disruptive

In a 2003 Harvard Business Review article, writers Gary Hamel and Liisa Välikangas defined resilience as "a capacity to undergo deep change without or prior to a crisis." People with that kind of foresight are rare. Most people don't see the need for change until a crisis forces them into it.

Sometimes crisis comes as a result of unforeseen circumstances, but crisis can also result from someone who is willing to risk disrupting the status quo. Shawn Fanning created a disturbance in the entertainment industry with the first file-sharing application known as Napster in 2002. Former NFL player Colin Kaepernick disrupted our social awareness by kneeling for the National Anthem in 2016. Without those who are willing to cause disruption, we might very well still be living in the Stone Age.

 When all is well, with two cars in every garage and a chicken in every pot, disruption is not only unwelcome, it might very well be unnecessary. Is it fair to say that comfort is the enemy of innovation?

 Those who are satisfied with the status quo abhor disruption. Why wouldn't they? No one wants to go through the difficulty of change if they see no need for it. The challenge comes when the status quo that rewards many in a society, also creates pain for others. Change is for those who find the status quo oppressive or unfair and it often takes a disruptor to get those in the majority to understand the plight of those who have been left out.

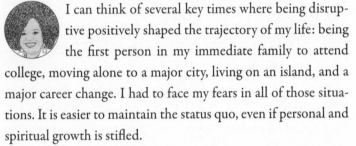 I can think of several key times where being disruptive positively shaped the trajectory of my life: being the first person in my immediate family to attend college, moving alone to a major city, living on an island, and a major career change. I had to face my fears in all of those situations. It is easier to maintain the status quo, even if personal and spiritual growth is stifled.

The concern of innovative trailblazers is about creating or experiencing something new or sourcing a new solution to a challenge. When Rosa Parks refused to move to the back of the bus in Montgomery, Alabama, comfort was not her goal. When Richard and Mildred Loving, an interracial couple from Virginia, were arrested in defiance of the law in 1958, comfort was not the goal. When Colin Kaepernick decided to kneel in protest of police brutality in the African-American community, comfort was not a guiding force in his behavior. They wanted to disrupt a pattern or a precedent. They wanted change, justice, and to confront society's dark tendencies.

Most disruption rises from a long held deep ache in the pit of the belly that won't go away until it's resolved. For many looking in from the outside, the actions may seem sudden, even problematic, but the underlying issues have been boiling for a long time. When I began the long journey of examining my life in religious traditions and fundamentalism, it seemed sudden and rushed to those who knew me. They didn't understand that I had been spiritually uncomfortable and pondering questions for an extended period, literally decades. The personal decision to move forward into a more relational understanding of God cost me some relationships. Some walked out of my life simply because I chose to leave a denomination with which I no longer aligned. It wasn't about comfort. I was already uncomfortable in my struggle to change as well as being uncomfortable in the relationships I lost.

 You understood the cost attached to each decision and you made the determination that whatever discomfort it caused initially, the results would be worth it. Isn't that always the catalyst? I think of my own journey as a frustrated pastor. Even though I knew something was wrong for a long time before, I stayed longer than I should have for the comfort of salary and my desire to meet other people's expectations. Often, we find ourselves making the best out of a bad situation, until we can't.

 I've had many disruptive moments that have shaped me, but probably none more impactful than reading the first few pages of *A New Kind of Christian,* a book by Brian McLaren. I reread those opening pages again and again—stunned that someone had so accurately articulated what I'd been thinking and feeling for years. I had struggled with a growing dissatisfaction with the business of religion and the subsequent demands it had placed on me. As you said, Arnita, the seeds of disruption had been present for years on the inside, but the words I read caused those seeds to grow to a point where I found the courage to make changes.

The Personal Challenge of Disruption

 Although I fully comprehend the historical realities of church and segregation, I never understood why Sunday morning segregation is so acceptable *now*.

Why does the church not have a stronger desegregation stance? I have noticed on videos of church services how the camera often shows the minority culture of that church body. When I made the conscious, prayerful decision to step away from an African-American church and move to a predominantly white community of faith, closer to my home, I was a disruptor, even though *my mind* was not completely settled in the decision. I had been comfortable in the African-American church, as that was my heritage.

When I had visited a similar church earlier, I invited my spiritual father to come with me. After the service, he spoke frankly with me. He said that I was doing something that he himself could not do. I was leaving behind all that was familiar and making a choice to immerse myself—and my family—in a foreign cultural church experience. I was willfully entering an arena where there would be pressure to conform to whiteness, suburban norms, values, and, of course, worship expression.

One time, a member of a white church I attended was annoyed by my saying "Amen" out loud during the service. This was common for me from my heritage, but uncommon for him. A dear white friend from the church found out about his complaint and said to me: "Do not let white people turn you into them!" Well, there it was!

I know a radical choice like that is not for everyone, but I felt compelled to be a bridge between races even though doing so placed me on a bit of an island and demolished my comfort zones. There were significant costs involved from both sides of the racial divide. It was even difficult to find those with whom I could discuss the journey because the journey was not common and was easily misunderstood.

I certainly didn't see my decision to engage a Muslim leader as disruptive or innovative, I simply saw it as the right thing to do. I meet with all types of people. I collect friends in the same manner that others might collect coins. My circle is large, but it has certainly gotten a bit smaller as I've engaged the Muslim community. The shrinking of that circle wasn't my choice.

For me, the choice was simple. I was engaging a friend whose experiences were not like mine. And, by nature, I'm curious to hear the stories of others who aren't like me. That decision to engage has certainly come with cost.

 When I began pursuing common ground thinking with others, I was simply a parent volunteer who had no experience with school administration. Even though I wasn't an expert, I was a pastor in the community. The party line said that public schools were dangerous for our children so we had to only consider private Christian schools or homeschooling.

For me, it didn't make sense to say God had been expelled from public schools. Where my children attended, 70 percent of the teachers were Christians. When national advocacy groups were perpetrating lies, I felt someone should at least tell the truth. In this case, it was speaking truth to my own community, which had been convinced that public schools were determined to lead our children down the path to atheism.

I also discovered that financial interests often run in the opposite direction of disruptive innovation. Once, a man attended one of my workshops—he was a leading advocate for every Christian child to abandon public schools by a targeted date. Afterward, he told me that the workshop had changed him, calling it the best thing he had ever heard. Thinking that his influence could help build bridges to our public schools and since he showed such an enthusiastic willingness to learn, I spent more time with him.

A few months later, he was invited to speak in Texas and asked for my curriculum. I was happy to have the message heard everywhere, so I gave him what he needed. After his appearance in Texas, he released a newsletter that, once again, was filled with fear tactics encouraging parents to pull their children from public schools. After I read it, I called him and asked why he had reverted to his old form. After speaking about common ground, he told me, his donations had dropped by 90 percent, so he had to go back to the message his base wanted to hear. Unfortunately, there's not much to gain financially in the area of peacemaking.

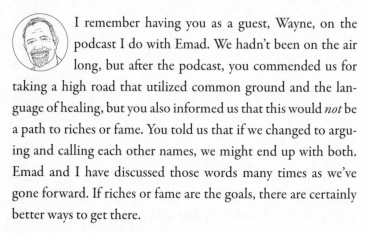 I remember having you as a guest, Wayne, on the podcast I do with Emad. We hadn't been on the air long, but after the podcast, you commended us for taking a high road that utilized common ground and the language of healing, but you also informed us that this would *not* be a path to riches or fame. You told us that if we changed to arguing and calling each other names, we might end up with both. Emad and I have discussed those words many times as we've gone forward. If riches or fame are the goals, there are certainly better ways to get there.

Disruption Can Be Positive

Although most people will attribute a negative connotation to someone being disruptive, I can see a potential positive result. For most people, it will take some level of disruptive behavior for personal life change.

We easily fall into rote patterns, especially in our relationships. We see the same people again and again. We walk into a room and gravitate toward the familiar, but we have much to gain by reaching outside our mundane circle of experiences. It may look like asking the Muslim leader of your community for his phone number or stepping away from a lifetime of cultural traditions into the unknown experiences of another ethnic group.

Disruption is a powerful intention to simply take a risk to upset patterns in hopes of discovering something new. Of course, there's also part of my personality that loves to explore unconventional ways of seeing things because I believe there is normally more than one way to see most things. I am not afraid to challenge something untrue or of the value judgments others project on me. I am acutely aware that many people see any challenge contrary to their way or perspective as disruptive. This positions them for a growth opportunity.

One thing I know for sure, the results to my life of being disruptive have been so worth the initial discomfort and awkwardness. I met people who preferred me and some who did not. Usually the feeling was mutual. I learned how to put myself in the shoes of others, and I realized how complex life can be. My network of friends increased substantially, and now I cannot imagine my life without so many incredibly different people. I learned more about myself—both strengths and weaknesses—and I received a deeper sense of destiny.

It makes me think of giving birth, which is incredibly uncomfortable—but when you see your baby, the discomfort fades. I would not trade any part of this.

 We are not talking about disruption simply for the sake of disrupting. The kind of disruption we're talking about comes when you see such an injustice that you simply can't remain silent. When your soul is stirred, disruption nearly always follows. At that point, you become willing to endure whatever consequences might come your way because there's nothing more joyful than living at rest in your soul.

Whether positively or negatively, how we live shapes people around us. One of my favorite books is *People of the Lie* by M. Scott Peck. It does a great job exposing how dysfunctional people control those around them through lies and manipulation with the intent of creating fear and subservience, rather than promoting openness and honesty. Their purpose is to protect their own power.

Healing never results from lies! I have seen passive acceptance as a close relative to lies. The fight to be yourself is disruptive! People who speak the language of healing can recognize difference and uniqueness and give others permission to be unique. You might eat asparagus on Thanksgiving while I'm making collard greens. I stopped choosing to jump through hoops and pretending simply to make others happy. Forfeiting my unique identity is simply too high a price to pay.

Most of my life I've sadly done just the opposite. Until maybe ten years ago, I was whoever you needed me to be. You need someone to lighten the mood, I can be the funny guy. You need answers to the deep questions, I used to know *literally* everything, or at least pretended I did. These days, I have more questions than conclusions, so I'm the guy who is willing to say, "I don't know," when I'm asked tough questions.

The crazy thing is, as I've let go of my need to be liked by everyone, I've discovered more of who I really am. The realization that I'm not everyone's favorite flavor has been a worthy journey, but this authenticity makes me a better friend. And I'm convinced that those who successfully disrupt have a pretty good handle on who they are.

 I once flew across the country to speak at a retreat. The first night I was there, the pastor spoke. He was perhaps the most manipulative leader I had ever witnessed, and it was obvious to me that he was using my message of living loved to cast a veneer over his oppressive ways. It was so bad that I made the decision to leave.

The next morning, I asked the pastor if we could talk and told him I thought I'd been invited under false pretenses. When I said I was planning on leaving, he wasn't happy. "You're the keynote speaker," he said. "You can't leave." He proceeded to tell me that I wouldn't be paid a dime if I left and that he would not even cover my airfare.

I told him I was willing to stay, but also outlined what I would share about manipulation and guilt from false teachers. He immediately told me that I needed to go—right then!

Enhance the Freedom of Others

 One of the inevitable effects of disruptive innovation is a reshuffling of your friends. When we change our priorities, we will often lose relationships. In my case, it's never intentional. My friends are in my life as long as they want to be. Well, that's mostly true. I had a longtime friend who simply became a bit too toxic in the areas of religion and politics and it spilled over into our relationship. Sadly, I chose to step away rather than continue on a path that did nothing but frustrate both of us.

Thankfully, the journey includes new relationships that have formed as I've intentionally raised the volume and speak for those who often are unable to speak for themselves. I now live with more clarity and less fear. Doing what's right carries cost, but it's also a wonderful way to discover who "your people" truly are.

I recently initiated a social media dialogue about the importance of disruption, using Colin Kaepernick as an example. Did I lose friends that day? Yes. But a dear woman from Washington wrote me and said that my courage had given her permission to speak up. To that point, she said that she had simply been afraid. Our actions can spur others. Courage is contagious. As the late Nelson Mandela said, "To be free is not merely to cast off one's chains, but to live in a way that respects and enhances the freedom of others." That is disruption dipped in love.

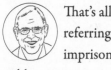 That's all the more powerful when you realize he was referring to his oppressors—the very ones who had imprisoned him. He was fresh out of prison with public sentiment on his side and backed by an overwhelming black majority in South Africa. Alongside Archbishop Desmond Tutu they showed a country that none of us are free until we're *all* free.

It would have been easy for those who had been oppressed to take over and become oppressors. It has happened many times, even in nearby African countries. However, they had the foresight to know it wouldn't serve anyone well.

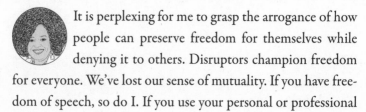 It is perplexing for me to grasp the arrogance of how people can preserve freedom for themselves while denying it to others. Disruptors champion freedom for everyone. We've lost our sense of mutuality. If you have freedom of speech, so do I. If you use your personal or professional

platform for your opinion, so can I. Arrogance rejects objectivity and seeks unquestioned agreement.

Individuals who fight for justice are rarely popular. Those who pursue deep levels of truth are rarely popular. If we really desire freedom personally or collectively, we have to hold a high regard for truth even if doing so results in persecution or rejection.

•

Try This

Crawl: *Be careful not to use being a disruptor as an excuse to be a jerk by yelling, name-calling, and interrupting others in your conversations.*

Walk: *When you realize that people you know either misunderstand or are belittling the views of another, is it difficult for you to risk those relationships to help them learn something helpful? If so, why?*

Run: *Set aside a time to visit an unfamiliar place void of your normal crowd. Just sit there for fifteen to thirty minutes. If you dare, talk to someone different.*

SECTION 3

Operating in Shared Space

We all have preferences of belief and action that we can freely live out in the privacy of our lives and our associations. However, a representative democracy asks us to cooperate in the shared spaces of our society, rather than co-opt them for one point of view over another.

Learning to operate generously in these shared spaces will allow us to build that "more perfect union," not because we all agree, but because we respect one another beyond our disagreements. None of our political parties, media, lobbyists, or political action committees help us fight for this shared space. It will take the generosity of ordinary citizens to build this space to enrich all of our lives.

11

Disarming the Binary Bomb

———————————◉———————————

In 2018, More in Common released a study called "The Hidden Tribes of America" that documented how most of our polarization is being fomented and funded by 6 percent of the population that they designated as the Progressive Activists and 27 percent of the population that they called the Traditional and Devoted Conservatives. Their amplification of our political issues has created a binary approach, where someone has to be completely right and the other has to be completely wrong.

The good news is that the rest of the population, nearly two-thirds—termed the Exhausted Majority—are tired of the vitriol, reject the binary options offered by those on the extreme, and want a more civil discussion of the issues that get to more nuanced and effective solutions.

This is the place where the language of healing can be most effective. It will not deter those on the extremes, but it can give a language for the Exhausted Majority to find not only each other but also better options for the issues that confound us. We can disarm the binary bomb that politicians and media have been handing us for decades and invite the kind of conversations that will heal our divide rather than perpetuate it. To do that we will have to move beyond binary thinking and invite others to reject the contrived options the extremists use to turn on each other.

When my kids were little, I wanted them to learn the beauty of choice and option. So I would give them two choices: you can have green beans or broccoli, mashed potatoes or a baked potato. Giving them binary choices was an easy, safe way of teaching them to think and make decisions. Neither choice was right or wrong, but better or best.

What served us well in childhood, however, can be more problematic when we move beyond eating or entertainment options. As we get older, choices become more complex and rarely can the issues of our society be fairly hammered into binary options. Yes, murder is wrong and there may be only one right answer to a math problem, but there are multiple options to untangle our immigration problem.

Elections, however, teach us otherwise. They force us to choose between A and B. There may be third party candidates, but rarely are they viable, so on election day most people vote to choose the lesser of two evils, or the platform they most prefer. In times past, our elected officials would move beyond the party platforms to govern effectively with those in the opposing party. Now, they don't even try.

Binary options about important issues are a limited way to think. All I have to do is choose between two options and my decision has been made. Often, this way automatically gives me a group to belong to. It's easier, with less conflict internally. It allows me to rush to certainty, without doing the harder work of considering other options or nuances, and thinking it through.

That's why so many are easily seduced into binary thinking. They think every issue can be simplified into an A or a B option, right or wrong. Too many people take in news from one media perspective that heightens this problem. Each morning, I go to Fox News, CNN, and the *LA Times* for my news. For me, diverse information sources give me more options to consider and a wider scope of what's going on in the world. When we splinter into binary thinking our thought process becomes narrower.

We see that play out every day in Supreme Court hearings, elections, and news coverage, where people jump to conclusions they were encouraged to reach, often on very little information. By making things binary and fomenting animosity toward the "other side," those in power have learned to control the populace, even as they polarize the country.

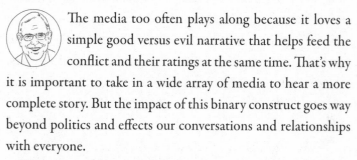

The media too often plays along because it loves a simple good versus evil narrative that helps feed the conflict and their ratings at the same time. That's why it is important to take in a wide array of media to hear a more complete story. But the impact of this binary construct goes way beyond politics and effects our conversations and relationships with everyone.

We see people around us in binary terms. I agree with them or I disagree. I am right, they are wrong. But few issues provide only an A or B option. We are really offered A to Z options and we ignore a whole set of permutations between B and Y that might offer a sweet spot to help us resolve our issues or personal disagreements.

The Power of Simultaneous

Reality is nuanced; so is wisdom. Mature thinkers can look beyond binary constructs and become multidimensional. If I look at my life and the issues I face, common sense and wisdom tell me that the options are probably greater than the two I might see initially, or even the one I prefer. My way isn't the only possibility. Binary thinking is diversity averse.

People tend to become multidimensional thinkers when the issues become more personal or close to home. It's easy to think in mutually exclusive options when we're not personally affected by the outcome. When the issue impacts us, we tend to flex our position. You can judge pregnant teenagers until your daughter comes home pregnant. That always appears as hypocrisy to me, but it may not be that at all. It may just be the first time another consideration became valuable.

 As gay rights became a flashpoint of controversy in the early 2000s, you didn't hear Vice President Dick Cheney say a word while in office. Why was that? He has a daughter named Mary who was in a same-sex relationship. His personal attachment caused him to view the issue different-ly, with a bit more nuance than even his political party would allow.

 Most people wouldn't buy a new car by only consid-ering two options. In our personal lives, most people are not binary thinkers, and yet we fall for it in so many cultural issues.

A friend of mine, whom I've known since he was two years old and is now in his twenties, posted on his social media feed during the 2016 election that if any of his friends said one posi-tive thing about Donald Trump, he would unfriend them—for life. If the goal is to stir up activity on your social media feed, it rewards simplistic, vitriolic, over-nuanced thinking, but the ensuing debate is worthless. We lose the conversation when ex-treme voices stake out mutually exclusive positions.

Sometimes I share P. J. O'Rourke's frustrations about social media: "Who's bright idea was it to put every idiot in the world in touch with every other idiot?"

 I see this dynamic play out in any emotionally charged area. The binary thinker just wants their friends to think they're right. People who think along nuanced lines employ more breadth in thinking. They want solutions and can relax the binary framework. Do you want to appear right, or do you want to seek the best solution?

You would think the answer to that is common sense, but sometimes it isn't all that common. It's possible that two things can be true at the same time, even complementing each other. In 2017, for instance, a lot of things were going on with black men being shot by police. One day, I went over to a friend's house and I saw that she had a "Back the Blue" flag in her yard. Given the current climate, I was shocked. I wondered why she felt like she had to take sides here. I knew that if one of my sons had been shot by the police, she would have been one of the first people at my house to comfort me. For some reason, she wasn't able to put *my* kids in those cars.

We had a brief conversation about the flag. She took a strong position to back the blue no matter what. I explained that I can't back the blue if the blue is a vigilante with the power to kill people without cause. I am not anti-police: I deeply respect law enforcement and their daily sacrifices to our community; but I also realize their power can be abused.

Anyone who feels the need to pick a side in this fight is viewing it in binary terms. When you go down that road, you are almost always wrong yourself. You're taking a one-sided view of something from a limited perspective and convincing yourself that you are right. *The power of simultaneous* recognizes that you can generally support law enforcement while at the same time realize there's a problem when black kids are at risk in their own neighborhoods from either fearful or racist police.

"Black lives matter." The whole focus on this statement has been about what you just discussed. Against popular belief in some communities the idea that black lives matter and that all lives mattering can coexist. Yet, when one of those cultures is grieving, "All lives matter" is a heartless and insensitive response.

When I heard my friends respond, "All lives matter," I'm convinced they really believe it, or at least hope it's true. They don't recognize that in some places some lives matter less simply because of their race or where they live. We can't ignore that.

It is possible to say that I want a secure border, yet at the same time I recognize that some people have lived and worked here for twenty-five years—and we have all benefited from their labor while underpaying them. Can't we do something to legalize the presence of people like that? They have nothing to go back to in their former countries. You can care about that without advocating open borders. Whenever we ignore nuance, we cannot solve the problem.

It's like the old Miller Lite ads. "Tastes great! No, it's less filling!" The point was both points of view were true. They wanted you to believe it did taste better *and* was less filling. It's like viewing a sky near sunset. Someone looking east would describe the sky as deep blue, while someone looking west would see pink or orange. We often become contentious simply because we don't view something from the same perspective. I just spent time with someone with whom I've had some theological disagreements and I heard myself say, "How do you not see this?" Here's the truth—I'm just as guilty as anybody else.

 One way to move a conversation outside polarization is to ask some simple questions. "Have you ever considered... ?" Or, "Do you know what that sounds like?"
Most of the time when I ask a question like that people will respond, "I've never thought of it that way."

 "What does it feel like to be wrong?" asked *New Yorker* staff writer, Kathryn Schulz in her popular TED talk. The audience offered answers that orbited around feelings of humiliation or embarrassment.

Her answer was shocking. "Being wrong feels like being right." That's the problem, isn't it? Until we realize we're wrong, we feel very confident. Arrogance keeps us from even considering that we might not have all the answers and when we get defensive the tension only grows.

I was talking to someone last week who, because I didn't agree with his political views, started talking to me like I was on the other side of the issue. I stopped him and let him know that I wasn't on the other side of this issue. He couldn't understand it. If I wasn't on side A, I had to be on side B. I told him that I'm not on A or B. In fact, I reject the framework. I see value in the arguments of both sides and wish we would work together to create a good policy that encompasses all legitimate concerns. He looked at me, dumbfounded. "I've never known other options."

He speaks for too many people, I'm afraid. But when you give them the opportunity to think outside those options, people come alive with possibilities.

Expand Your Friendships

In order to defuse binary thinking as my default, I keep a lot of friends who think differently than I do. Because I am a scientist, I am educated to think critically. I normally consider these questions: What is the real question? What information do I need to acquire? What assumptions have I made? I can look at multiple options at one time to figure out which one fits best. I get to ask questions one-on-one or in a small group. The personal touch of being able to pull somebody to the side and say, "You know what? This is what I'm kicking around in my mind. Could you shed light on what you think here?" But you can't go to blows and fall out with them if you are not aligned.

I'm careful not to do that on social media, which invites lots of conflict and emotional reaction. People can be brutal. Sometimes, it feels like another type of civil war in text form.

And social media just magnifies it because vitriol is coin of the realm. Anger begets anger, so we actually empower the immature, the zealot, to have the vocal space in society. They become the ones staking out this very narrow ground and then invite others to either join them in lockstep or defy them. The middle is gone.

Do you remember the "Argument Clinic," a comedy sketch by *Monty Python's Flying Circus* about where a man pays money to have an argument? There are people who will do anything to have arguments. It's how they live. It's who they want to be. Conflict is everything to them. You just have to avoid those people. I guarantee you all three of us can think of someone like that.

●

Or many someones! But I don't spend time with them. I spend the bulk of my time with people who are honest thinkers. It's where I learn—when I can have reasoned conversations that don't require agreement for friendship. If all your friends are only binary thinkers, they will only reinforce your own prejudices and blind spots. Expand your friendships.

It's important to break patterns that limit our personal growth. I love the way Arnita continues to make the conscious decision to step into diverse cultures. When I choose to engage people who think like me it's like playing checkers. When I embrace people who are not, I'm learning how to play chess.

I love what Wayne did with BridgeBuilders. He is masterful at creating a third room where A and Z can come together and think outside the box for a greater solution. That can help defuse binary thinking.

Recently, I was at an impasse with Emad and had invited Wayne on our podcast. We had a plan for the show, but he turned the tables and began to ask *us* questions. That episode, being led by our guest, honestly transformed our relationship.

Wayne, how do you do it? You literally defused binary thinking and helped them work together—the evidence of a real peacemaker!

The first ingredient, and maybe the most important, is to find people who are willing to engage the process of listening to others. Usually A and Z people aren't helpful. But draw from that Exhausted Majority who are willing to look for nuanced solutions, and some amazing things can happen. These people have passionate views, but they aren't dismissive of those with differing views.

Incidentally, we don't allow paid advocates in the room. If they're paid to drive the fight, they don't want to resolve it. They want to use the process, win or lose, as fodder for their next fundraising letter, and in that sense a loss can even be better than a win for them. They will see nothing good in the other side.

Then, I try to humanize, so that each sees the other as a counterpart—parents and educators, not simply people with an agenda "I" don't like. We often fail to see those on the other side of an issue as people with the same hopes and fears we all have.

Third, we set a solution as the goal. Do we really want this conflict to perpetuate or do we want to find a solution that we can all celebrate? Maybe it won't be exactly what we each want, but we can reach some agreements that respect our differences and the environment we share. Obviously private groups don't need to reach such accords, but public entities ought to fight for a common good that the vast majority of citizens can rally behind. Not everyone wants to promote gay rights, but they can get behind an environment that is safe for everyone.

Fourth, once we agree on that goal, we then ask, "Where are we not meeting that goal?" That requires some research and some listening that not only gives the group good information but also helps them develop empathy.

Finally, we craft a solution together. It's an amazing thing to watch a group vote for a solution unanimously. It means they've done the hard work of exploring beyond A and B.

•
Try This

Crawl: *When you are with people who differ from you, salt your conversation with questions like, "What do you think about... ?" or "Your perspective is an interesting way of looking at that. Have you also considered... ?" and see what happens.*

Walk: *Describe a current situation you're involved in that is filled with seemingly unresolvable conflict. What other options are you not considering?*

Run: *Identify by name a person you can bring into a difficult conversation who will have a different perspective. Contact them to discuss specifics.*

12

Bust Up Your Bias

———————◗———————

Bias is a prejudice in favor of or against one thing, person, or group compared to another, usually in a way considered to be unfair.

The great poet T. S. Eliot once said, "We can at least try to understand our own motives, passions, and prejudices, so as to be conscious of what we are doing when we appeal to those of others. This is very difficult, because our own prejudice and emotional bias always seems to us so rational."

Bias influences almost every human interaction we have, and it is most insidious when we're least aware of it. Identifying our biases and disarming them is a critical component to employing the language of healing.

A few years back, as our nation was facing several racially tense and perplexing scenarios, one of my friends invited me to come and facilitate a candid conversation centered around the topic of race. She gathered thirty of her friends and neighbors. The time was both powerful and intense as we tackled the tough questions with which racial interactions confront us.

Following that event, I received other informal invitations to help others navigate similar discussions. They were rarely comfortable times—we explored bias and preconceived notions and assumptions—but they were always beneficial in establishing new levels of understanding.

If we are serious about speaking language that heals relationship gaps, it's important to first admit the bias that lives deep inside all of us. Yes, even you! It's a common denominator for the human race. If we don't honestly locate it in ourselves, we will stay lost in the fog that bias brings.

Owning Up to Bias

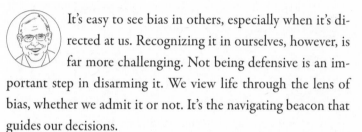 It's easy to see bias in others, especially when it's directed at us. Recognizing it in ourselves, however, is far more challenging. Not being defensive is an important step in disarming it. We view life through the lens of bias, whether we admit it or not. It's the navigating beacon that guides our decisions.

One look at social media or twenty-four-hour news is all we need to recognize its power over not just individuals, but also entire groups of people. Some proudly wear their bias like a badge of honor: This chapter is probably not for them. This is an opportunity for those who want to communicate beyond their bias.

The political landscape has always been a breeding ground for bias. In our present day, it's extremely rare to see a politician change their mind. The tendency is to dig in with the finest examples of truth bias, ignoring pesky facts as they adhere to the party line at all costs. It takes great courage to stand up for what's true when pressure is applied to do just the opposite. A few American presidents have shown the courage to do what's right in the face of opposition: Abraham Lincoln had his *Team of Rivals* as Doris Kearns Goodwin termed his cabinet, or when Lyndon Johnson ignored the noise from southern Democrats during the 1964 Civil Rights Act, for example. Those courageous acts, however, have become rare in today's culture.

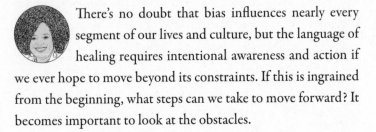 There's no doubt that bias influences nearly every segment of our lives and culture, but the language of healing requires intentional awareness and action if we ever hope to move beyond its constraints. If this is ingrained from the beginning, what steps can we take to move forward? It becomes important to look at the obstacles.

That's not easy in a culture preoccupied with externals, all of which create double standards and stereotypes. As men age, they are looked at as distinguished and wise. Women, on the other hand, are taught to fight the aging process to their last dollar.

Isn't it easy to make snap judgments often just by someone's appearance? I hate to admit it, but if someone cuts me off in traffic, or drives too slow or too erratically, I find myself looking to see who would drive like that. Whether it's an older driver or one from a different ethnicity or gender, I find myself jumping to conclusions that have no merit.

I'm sure that there are many who would dismiss that behavior—in which I also partake—as simply human nature, but I wonder if "human nurture" is a better term. This is learned behavior, even if we come by it honestly. So maybe the first step to becoming authentic and genuine is admitting that we might be a bit skewed in how we view others—often times due to how we view ourselves.

Bias inevitably leads to judgment, where healing and harmony become difficult. And it's rampant. When engaging someone in conversation for the first time, we nearly always ask the same question: "So, what do you do?" It seems like an innocent question, but it's as loaded as it gets. Please tell me what you do for a living so I can appraise where you fit on my scale of worth. To be completely transparent, doctors rank higher than me; laborers are below me. When I've asked that question during the years, it's been as much about my own value—my place—than anything else. During the past fifteen years or so, I've done my best to refrain from asking because even though I fight my own biases, I still fall short.

 Don't we see that in religious circles, as well? Every time we ask someone where they attend church, there are implicit judgments made. This becomes a detriment to communicating when our bias places others in a box where we no longer have to relate to them on an individual level.

If we are serious about finding a broad-based common ground, it is important to allow others to inhabit the same ground as us. And that's whether we view them above, below, or the same. I will admit to issues with people who are part of what I consider to be religiously oppressive groups. I find myself viewing them as religiously backward. Throughout my life, when I've seen those who dress a certain way due to their obligation, I've rolled my eyes with a bit of disgust. That disgust hasn't been directed toward individuals, but rather the system to which they adhere. So I've learned to put those feelings aside and still engage with the individual person.

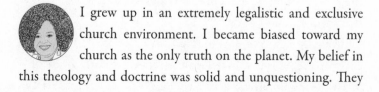 I grew up in an extremely legalistic and exclusive church environment. I became biased toward my church as the only truth on the planet. My belief in this theology and doctrine was solid and unquestioning. They

taught that God no longer speaks to us individually and nothing was said about the Holy Spirit or His gifts. In addition, only one group of people go to heaven.

At a certain point, if we want to move forward, we must address why we believe what we believe and our own arrogance. It's important to admit that our understanding might be flawed. After a change of heart and mind, I was ordained as a pastor at a charismatic church that believed that God still speaks and his gifts still operate today. It's a journey that I couldn't have imagined nor taken without addressing my bias. I know it is safe to say I would have missed part of my destiny without wrestling through my personal bias.

 I know I fight bias in many areas of my life. In my work with the poor and marginalized, for example, I oftentimes look sideways at the wealthy. I'm certainly not saying my bias is right or justifiable, but I can't deny that it's real. Most of the ministry I do, whether it be as Santa, giving toys to kids who are below the poverty line, or helping to rescue victims of human trafficking, the reality is that these are what the Bible refers to as "the least of these."

Does the income disparity in our culture bother me? If I'm honest, the answer is yes. I'm not making excuses, I'm just being a bit vulnerable. When I witness the desperation of the poor and contrast it with what often appears to be the condescension of many with wealth, it colors a large part of my thinking. In my case, I've found that my bias often correlates with wounds in my life, whether they be economic, religious, or otherwise. I suspect that's true for most of us.

Even though I've encountered many whose hearts match their wealth, this is still an area that I'm constantly aware of—and working on. There it is. Religious bias is alive and well in me. A local church implemented a marketing campaign years ago with hundreds of signs that simply read "I love my church." Innocent, right? Well, it made me go ballistic, but I'm not sure I wouldn't still have a similar reaction. I knew that they were referring to an institution with buildings, services, and programs—not a group of people who love. And that's a bias for me. I love people—institutions, not so much.

Being on the Receiving End of Bias

 Bias also comes at us. I often travel to impoverished areas. As an American, it is often assumed that I have wealth, and compared to them that's certainly true. Then they will attempt to ingratiate themselves to me—making sure that I am aware of their needs in order to sway me to help them financially.

Gender also comes into play. Because I am a man, I have to be aware of the impact I may have on women who fear for their safety. Something as innocent as walking my dog requires an extra bit of navigation. I was recently walking behind a woman while taking our dog for a walk at twilight. As I approached her from behind, I was careful to simply say, "Hello ma'am. I'm passing you with my dog." She thanked me, even though I could sense that she felt a bit threatened.

 Those that are biased against me have likely come by it honestly. I can be opinionated and even brash, which creates a bit of reputation. I have a friend who provides video production services for many political campaigns in central California. He recently told me that my name often comes up in those political circles—and usually in a negative way. He told me that those comments make him respect me at a higher level, but there's a part of me that is saddened. I now find myself working a bit harder to undo some of their misconceptions, even if they were honestly earned.

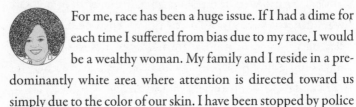 For me, race has been a huge issue. If I had a dime for each time I suffered from bias due to my race, I would be a wealthy woman. My family and I reside in a predominantly white area where attention is directed toward us simply due to the color of our skin. I have been stopped by police officers on several occasions and it's always the same question: "Do you live around here?" My address is on my license! Someone actually called the police on my husband while he was walking in our neighborhood. My sons have been called the "n-word" on multiple occasions. I shop in local retail stores where I've received "extra attention" from the employees, who are always watching me with undue surveillance.

I've been complimented on being so articulate, as well as having well-behaved children, as if that is surprising instead of normal. At our local polling precinct, my identity was questioned, even though they had my driver's license and voter registration in their hands!

In my opinion, bias is the very root of racial profiling and discrimination. From my experience, nothing on earth provokes a biased response more than skin tone.

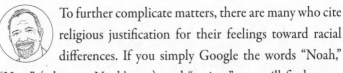 To further complicate matters, there are many who cite religious justification for their feelings toward racial differences. If you simply Google the words "Noah," "Ham" (who was Noah's son), and "racism," you will find something known as "The Curse of Ham." As the story is told in Genesis 9, Noah had overindulged in wine, causing him to lay naked in his tent while drunk. His son, Ham—who was the father to a son named Canaan—told his brothers, who then covered their father.

Upon awakening, Noah condemned Ham's behavior and pronounced a curse upon Ham's son, Canaan, saying that he would be a servant to his brothers. As far as Bible stories go, it's not out of the ordinary, but that story has been used throughout history to justify everything from slavery to genocide. The crazy thing is, the misinterpretation of Scripture did not come from careful examination of the text, but rather white Europeans looking for biblical justification for their supposed racial superiority.

There have been millions of people led down this abhorrent ideology over the course of time. Some used the "Mark of Cain," who murdered his brother, Abel. There are those who have interpreted the marking of Cain as black skin. Latter Day Saints used the story of Cain to exclude black men from the priesthood until 1978, when a new "revelation" came to them. When religion is used to further racial agendas, it's insidious. And it leads to bias, which is the root of racism.

 I have never heard this, and it really, really unnerves. Maybe that's partly why Sunday morning is the most segregated time in our country.

I once visited a new church and, upon entering the building, was approached by a greeter who is there to *welcome* people to church. But his welcome for me was a bit different than for others. He thought I was in the wrong place. "The church you're looking for is up the street a bit," he said. I verified the name of the church and told him that I was indeed in the right place. I then watched from a distance and noted no one else was approached as they entered the building.

Why is there such fear and discomfort with black skin in a white neighborhood? In Oakland, California, a black fireman knocked on a door to perform a required city safety inspection, but when a neighbor saw him climbing a ladder to the roof—in his fireman's uniform—he still called 911. Stories abound of black people being reported to the police when entering their own home. Of necessity, I had to teach my sons that some people would dislike and treat them with suspicion simply due to the dark skin that God gave them.

Banishing Bias

 Conversations about race are uncomfortable. There seem to be pitfalls and traps everywhere. It's easy to say the wrong thing, offending others in the process. And saying the wrong words in today's culture can lead to finding yourself ostracized and unemployed. When we have discussed race among ourselves, we've had an element of safety, but that's due to your generosity, Arnita, and our growing relationship with one another. In that environment, questions can be asked without fear.

It's even gotten difficult for people to grow through their biases. In our hypervigilant society people find past statements on social media about race or sexual orientation and condemn the person in the present. If we can't be honest, we can't grow, and if we don't give people the freedom to grow, they'll give up trying to see the issue fairly.

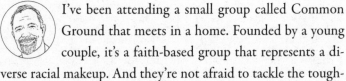 I've been attending a small group called Common Ground that meets in a home. Founded by a young couple, it's a faith-based group that represents a diverse racial makeup. And they're not afraid to tackle the toughest issues of our culture through the lens of healthy dialogue and an opportunity to learn. The first meeting centered around race. As the leader, Josh did not want to offend, so he first asked about

preferred racial terminology. "Do we call you black? African-American? Something else?" he asked. At first, I thought it was a bit over the top, but I recognized the wisdom in asking the question. It made us all laugh. And his questions were answered graciously by the half dozen black people in attendance that night. From there, we all knew that honest dialogue was in play.

 When our cultural exposure is narrow, it becomes easier to display bias. For instance, I know people who were denied entrance to the university of their choice or a job promotion, so they harbor bias toward an entire group of people due to what they perceive as affirmative action. Because of this bias, they conclude that the other person was less qualified and dwell on the perceived injustice. If the media portrays the majority of arrests involving those with darker skin, I'm more inclined to lump all who look like that into the same category. Our negative experiences—and negative exposure—confirm our bias. The antidote is to broaden our conversations and relationships with different people.

That means we will have to be intentional in our relational reach. My own pursuit of my friend, Emad, has diminished my personal biases. When I found out he drives a four-wheel vehicle and loves off-roading, I began to playfully call him a Muslim Redneck. He countered with, "I'm more American than you are." My heart has been changed simply by exposure. I've found good and bad in every race and culture. It's difficult to continue to walk in prejudice and bias when you have a personal relationship.

 Bias is deeply entrenched in our cultural experiences. Often, we adopt cultural bias simply from believing that the way we do things is the right way. That mind-set can cause conflict in relationships, marriages, and even work spaces. When I was living in St. Thomas in the U.S. Virgin Islands, a friend visited from Memphis. Wanting her to have the best experience, I took her to buy fish from a fisherman directly off a boat. I pointed out six fish to the man, who then wrapped them up and handed them to me. I just stood there, looking at the fish. They weren't filleted, so I handed them back. I could see the anger in the fisherman's eyes as he threw his knife on the ground while muttering, "Wasteful American." He filleted my fish and I paid him three times what the fish would normally cost. I then asked him to take the heads and tails home to his family to make soup. He gave me a half smile. I had insulted him with my unintentional cultural insensitivity, but we managed to find a place of peace.

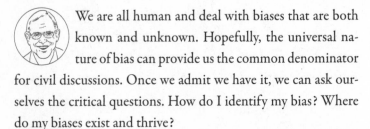 We are all human and deal with biases that are both known and unknown. Hopefully, the universal nature of bias can provide us the common denominator for civil discussions. Once we admit we have it, we can ask ourselves the critical questions. How do I identify my bias? Where do my biases exist and thrive?

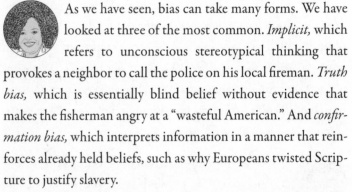 As we have seen, bias can take many forms. We have looked at three of the most common. *Implicit,* which refers to unconscious stereotypical thinking that provokes a neighbor to call the police on his local fireman. *Truth bias,* which is essentially blind belief without evidence that makes the fisherman angry at a "wasteful American." And *confirmation bias,* which interprets information in a manner that reinforces already held beliefs, such as why Europeans twisted Scripture to justify slavery.

Of course, with more than seven billion people on the planet, there are more than three types, but these three are a good place to start examining your own biases.

●

Try This

Crawl: *Understand that language has bias and see if you can remove language that is full of false assumptions and perpetuates stereotypes involving religion, sex, politics, gender, and race. For example, you would not say, "All black men..." "All Muslim women..." All Evangelical Christians..." All white women..." "All Mexican men..."*

Walk: *Out of the three biases in our discussion—implicit bias, truth bias, or confirmation bias—which one of these most inhibits your ability to relate to people who are different?*

Run: *Identify an area where you know you have bias and an area that you suffer from bias against you. The next time you are in a conversation that makes you uncomfortable, identify your bias.*

13

Sharing the Table

---◦---

"All great change in America begins at the dinner table." —President Ronald Reagan

Whether we're sharing food or sharing thought, the table has become a symbol of inclusion. In families, we learn to communicate and interact around the shared experience of sitting at the table. In business, a seat at the table is the equivalent of being heard. For many, the table is the first place where we learn our value—or lack thereof.

Healing or wounding—it can all be found at the table.

 The greatest challenge in building an equitable society is to find a way to share power with those groups who have been traditionally left out. For that to happen, those who already have a seat at the table have to make a path for those who do not.

History teaches us that humans don't share power well. Whoever has it, tends to grab on tightly, unwilling to share it with others for fear of losing their own advantage. They are usually under the misguided notion that they earned their way there and others can, too. That's why most of our progress on civil rights has sadly come from the courts, not the legislature.

This is not an easy process especially when an invitation to the table often conflicts with our own self-interests.

Cooperation Over Coercion

 I first heard the phase, "Cooperation is always prefer-able to coercion," when I saw a movie called *The Grey Fox*. Unfortunately, we live in a society that values holding on and holding out until the bitter end. It's the mental-ity that says you can have my "fill-in-the-blank" when you can pry it from my cold, dead hands. Few who hold power yield it without being forced.

I once advocated for a young woman who had been an abuse victim within a very large religious denomination. She was sim-ply seeking a small amount of money to obtain counseling, but the denomination told me that, while they were sympathetic, they had never written a check without first being forced by a binding, legal decision.

After the woman filed a lawsuit, that denomination ended up paying nearly a hundred times more than the original amount she had asked for. And, of course, that was only after a legal or-der. Unfortunately, whether we're talking about a religious orga-nization helping an abuse victim with counseling or even *Brown vs. Board of Education*, tragically, change rarely occurs without compulsion.

 I am a woman of color who was born in the 1960s, and I've seen doors open that were the sole result of legal decisions. Those changes, however forced they may have been at the time, have positively shifted the culture. The right thing to do is still the right thing to do, regardless of how it was achieved. In matters of change, whether it's a govern-ment, corporation, or even a sports team, change is nearly always slow, evolutionary, and resisted.

•

Sometimes change is a product of legal decisions, but society can bring that same pressure. We've seen cultural changes between men and women through the Me Too movement. In the case of baseball, we saw the Brooklyn Dodgers sign and play Jackie Robinson, but the world was changing and there were societal pressures that Dodgers president, Branch Rickey, had to weigh. But still, someone had to be first.

I went to college with a man named Otis Young who costarred in a television Western called *The Outcasts*. He was the very first African-American actor to receive top billing as a cowboy on TV—way back in 1968. But again, attitudes were shifting and Hollywood understood that backlash was imminent if they didn't expand opportunities for minorities to sit at the table. Today, we routinely see works of art on the screen from black directors like Spike Lee or Ava DuVernay, but those opportunities are available due to sacrifices from trailblazers like Melvin Van Peebles. Someone always has to go first.

 When we are forced to share our public spaces, it often leads to sharing our private spaces. When doors open publicly, it has been a catalyst to invite those who aren't like me into my private spaces that I choose to share. The details that drive change at the beginning, regardless of motivation, often lead to great outcomes—especially when it leads to us relating to one another in deeper, better ways.

 Sadly, coercion is nearly always the way it has to be done. This goes beyond race. At its root, it is about power. In the political arena, there is little motivation to share the table with someone who doesn't subscribe to the same ideological line of thought. If I allow a dissenting voice into my space, my voice is diluted. That's why people want to exclude voices that threaten their preferred way of life.

In many cases, this is about something as primal as family. Many can't allow the differing opinions of outside voices to disrupt the status quo. At times, that can have a racial component, especially when it comes to issues like housing or the bussing of schoolchildren. Incubating a desire for what's best for the community as a whole—the common good—can be a real uphill battle.

Here's where my understanding is lacking. In the United States, we like to talk about equality. We're quick to say that all people are created equal. They are. If that's truly the case, why is it nearly impossible to provide equal access to the table? There's a real problem when what we espouse doesn't line up with what we believe and subsequently demonstrate. If we truly believe those lofty words about equality, we won't have an issue with sharing power. This is a human conundrum. Perhaps, it is time to build a bigger table!

So you're saying that talk is cheap?

Seriously, it's pitiful that it has taken so long for the majority culture to embrace sharing the table. I'm sorry for how long people like you have been kept from utilizing the fullness of your insights and creativity. Instead, we have been content to say that opportunities exist for all who are willing to work for them. "If I got a seat at the table, so can you. Nothing is holding you back." They mean the law allows it, but they haven't equalized the opportunities to get you there. Historic inequities have led to chronic disparities in our culture. Where is the compassion that kicks down the barriers and opens up the table to those who are underrepresented?

There's certainly an element of first use, for lack of a better term—simply those who have had a historical place at the table. And while all may be welcome, few are ever invited. The thought becomes, "Go ahead. If you can get here, we aren't going to stop you. But it's not our responsibility to help." For the common good, we have to invite and include those who are not like us.

Being Tolerated Is Not Enough

 It's not enough to hear people say that I'm included especially when it's not the palpable reality. Being tolerated is not the same as being included. I'm worth more than just being tolerated. I am not a whiner or a beggar for the attention of those in power. I have something to offer. At times, it is frustrating to have to sit back and wait for an invitation.

 If the invitation *never* arrives, by all means, push your way in. Sometimes, we don't recognize our blind spots. I was recently preparing a blog for publication on WordPress when they sent a message encouraging me to add captions to my photos. Well, that involved a fair amount of extra work simply to increase visibility, but then I read through the notice. It said, "The visually impaired will not know what the photo is without a description." What I perceived as a request in the self-interest of WordPress was actually about a group of people who would be underserved without captions.

Some are simply left out and, without real understanding, will always be excluded. It may seem like an insignificant incident, but it had a huge impact on me. I didn't realize that a small amount of work for me could equal a better experience for someone else.

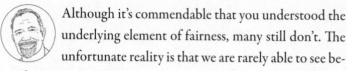 Although it's commendable that you understood the underlying element of fairness, many still don't. The unfortunate reality is that we are rarely able to see beyond our own needs as our bottom line becomes solely how things affect us. In the Bible, this is well illustrated by the story of The Good Samaritan. One by one, people were too busy to stop and help someone who had literally been injured during a crime. The victim was traveling through an area when he was assaulted, stripped, and beaten. The story may have been different had he been a local resident, but he was simply passing through. The story says that two professional clergy members chose to cross the street and ignore the man's plight. But another outsider—a mixed-race Samaritan—felt compassion and, at a fair amount of personal expense, helped the man recover.

Perhaps the key to changing our hearts has to first come in how we view others. It took an outsider to help another stranger. What would happen if we simply began to view others through the lens of those who are not like us?

The Power of Diversity

Because I am a leadership coach, I am often approached by companies and individuals about diversity concerns. I tell them that diversity requires a new way of thinking. We need to become comfortable with being uncomfortable. That's the reality. Change is never comfortable. Speaking the language of healing will not be easy. It requires intentional thought and actions.

In the corporate world, whether it's private or public, the shift has to begin at the top senior levels. Hiring practices have to be made on an equitable basis. It has to begin there. Without that, the cycle of diminishing those who are different will continue. We can always invite others into our private spaces, but true diversity and inclusion will always run along power lines in organizations. Invitations matter. Is it possible to force your way in? Maybe, but that is nearly always met with resentment and a social exclusion. As a result, you may indeed find yourself at the table, but still without a voice. How disappointing!

 Arnita, knowing you has changed my life. I look at things through a different lens because of our friendship. I was at a charity golf tournament the other day and when I finished walking through the food line, I turned to see open seats at two tables. Four Caucasians were sitting at one and three African-Americans were at the other. I didn't know anyone at either table.

Before you, I know which I would have chosen just because I'd feel less awkward. This time, however, I wanted to sit at the other table and explore some new relationships, and I was glad that I had.

I've always thought of myself as a man who treats all people equally, but after knowing you, Arnita, I'm finding myself much more aware, and much more intentional. Recently, I heard from a woman who has read and been impacted by a few of my books. Since she's in the Los Angeles area, she contacted me and asked if we could meet. My wife, Sara, and I agreed to meet her for dinner at a restaurant.

She called ahead to tell me that she was wearing a purple sweater so we could spot her. I also knew she was a woman of color and told her we'd have no trouble spotting her since there were no others like her in the room. She had a good laugh at that, and it opened the door for us to discuss openly and freely some of her experience with race. She had been raised in Louisiana and told stories of how her family faced discrimination there.

Before this project, I would have definitely been more timid and more careful in my conversation. That dinner was a far more rewarding experience due to spending time with you.

My worldview has changed as a result of the difficult conversations that we've chosen to engage. You two have made no effort to change who I am or morph my difference. Neither of you have forced me to have a white, male, suburban perspective in our discussions. True diversity requires inclusion. True inclusion means that I can come to the table and not be like you—I can just be me. So on every level this has been an inclusive experience. I am grateful for that. Anything less than that would have made me feel like a token.

When we expect others to come to the table and be like us or know their place, that's tokenism. Who wants to come to the table without authenticity? We all have the power to be catalysts for true inclusion. With my background in chemistry, I find the word *catalyst* fascinating. In chemistry, a catalytic agent is often added to an environment to produce significant change, yet the agent itself does not change at all. Whether it accelerates or slows down a reaction, it always produces an effect. Catalysts produce change. Be a catalyst. Bring others to the table.

I love the concept that different chemicals, when they're combined, can create something entirely new and different. It's like the mystery of marriage—two becoming one. With my friend Emad, we've been able to go from "you and me" to "we." That's the direct result of two disparate people coming together and making the conscious decision just to spend time with each other. We found both friendship and intimacy at the table. Two elements can be brought together to create something new, which is how change works.

In a book I wrote called *Finding Church*, I purposely used the word *catalyst* to describe what the best of church leadership can be. Instead of casting a vision and getting people to follow them, real leaders inspire others to their better ambitions. As they change, they will impact their communities.

Moving Forward

 I'm convinced that the major component keeping us from inclusiveness is fear. Fear is a powerful motivator that operates along every culture and socioeconomic reality. It's the great equalizer that keeps us all in line, whether it be the fear of failure or the fear of losing what we have.

Why is it so difficult to invite others to the table? We don't want to lose any of our power, prestige, or money. When we invite different thoughts to the table, we run the very real risk of losing it all: That's what fear tells us. If we can get to the point where our desire for better outcomes pulls ahead of our fear, we can effect change. Until then, we are content with things staying exactly where they are.

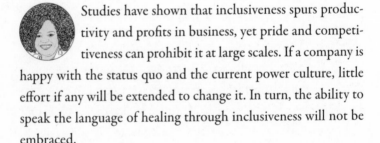 Studies have shown that inclusiveness spurs productivity and profits in business, yet pride and competitiveness can prohibit it at large scales. If a company is happy with the status quo and the current power culture, little effort if any will be extended to change it. In turn, the ability to speak the language of healing through inclusiveness will not be embraced.

 So those of us who can must begin to be the catalysts. There are many who are ready for change and there are many who are willing to lead the way. Those who are only looking for their share—the "what's in it for me" crowd—will always be with us. But many people are looking beyond their personal needs and desires to the common good of the community. That's my hope.

•

Try This

Crawl: *When you extend an invitation for someone different to join you at the table, make it personal and ensure that your tone and nonverbal cues are welcoming and sincere.*

Walk: *Within your circle of influence, how do you feel about challenging your own comfort zone and being a catalyst to invite difference to the table?*

Run: *Be an advocate for inclusion within the power structures you encounter. Inclusion welcomes diverse perspectives and thought and not just obvious difference like race and gender.*

Friendly Fire

"When a man is hit by friendly fire, his blood pressure lowers and his morale sinks. I have been hit by friendly fire in my heart. Sighs spill from my body instead of blood." —Hideo Kojima

There's an old saying that simply says, "Friendly fire isn't." Those words reflect the reality of wounds that are inflicted by those closest to us. And there's very little about it that's friendly, even though it's often accompanied by smiles or even good intentions. The truth is this: Pain is always deeper when it comes from those we know, love, and respect.

The phrase *friendly fire,* which found its origins in military jargon, nearly always refers to *accidentally* harming those who are your allies, whether it be by words or actions. Unfortunately, some people extend the definition to include those close to us who *intentionally* wound. But in fact, greater proximity often leads to greater pain.

During a recent conversation with a friend about transgendered use of public restrooms, I suggested compassion for those who have a perception of their gender that falls outside the majority. I was immediately scolded. "Why is it that you love transsexuals more than you love Christians?" In an instant, I'd been identified as an enemy. Why can't I love them both? He saw the issue as a zero-sum game, demanding that I choose one or the other. Normally, words like that don't bother me, but this isn't just a friend—he is a close friend who knows me well. It seemed to me the political fight was more important than our friendship.

 All three of us have chosen paths that are often outside the mainstream—at least as far as those closest to us are concerned. Arnita, you stepped out of life-long religious tradition with the intent of expanding your world.

Wayne began asking hard questions about the institutions of church and religion. I associate with and deeply love Muslims and those who struggle with issues of sexuality. In our inner circles, those decisions have opened us to criticism and judgment from those closest to us.

When you begin to question the status quo, friendly fire is often the result. In the interest of full disclosure, I can't tell you how many times I've voiced my thoughts only to hear someone say, "You're just speaking out of your wounds." I've heard those words from people closest to me, who have known me for more than twenty years! By attributing my current views to some past moment of pain, they can dismiss them. I freely admit to having a chip on my shoulder about some of the things I've been through, but that accusation stops the conversation dead in its tracks. It's often impossible to convince friends or colleagues that our thoughts weren't birthed in wounds. Wounds don't always make us bitter; sometimes they make us wiser.

Words That Wound

 Friendly fire has been around a while. In Psalm 55, David said that he could endure the insults of an enemy, but he was stung by the rejection of a man with whom he had enjoyed a close friendship. In my own life, there have been times that I've been vulnerable with those I've trusted, only to have those words later used against me to discredit me. And I'm not sure we can honestly look at friendly fire without considering the mix of religion and politics. I've got friends who believe a Christian can't possibly be a Democrat. I've got other friends who believe a Christian can't be a Republican. What they have in common is that all genuine Christians would adhere to the same political ideology—theirs!

As one Republican politician told me recently, "I'm wondering if it wouldn't be easier for me to be a pro-life Democrat, than a compassionate Republican."

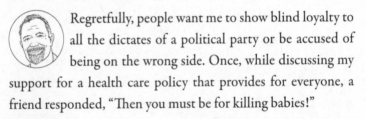

Regretfully, people want me to show blind loyalty to all the dictates of a political party or be accused of being on the wrong side. Once, while discussing my support for a health care policy that provides for everyone, a friend responded, "Then you must be for killing babies!"

My experience with friendly fire is closer to the military definition, where the fire isn't intentional. It comes from people making thoughtless statements without malice or consciousness. A church friend once asked my son why he didn't just "date his own kind."

Obviously, this friend was close enough to feel comfortable asking the question, but he didn't even consider the meaning behind it. I'm not even sure he understood that his question was hurtful. When it comes to the impact of their words, some people are just clueless. Over the years, I've been told that I'm "beautiful... for a black woman." Or that I'm "smart... for a black woman." An African-American friend of mine invited a white woman to her home. When she walked in, she commented with surprise, "Wow! Your house is so clean." That's friendly fire. There's no intent to injure, but it's nearly always the outcome.

Friendly fire constantly occurs in marriage. We all have a tendency to say things to our spouses without understanding the full impact of our words, or even how they are being heard. Once we understand their impact, however, we can be careful to not repeat the language that wounds, which is why gentle honesty is important to a growing relationship. In order to speak the language of healing, our society must have the same understanding. We recognize where we have hurt and wounded one another and simply do better as we go forward.

 One of my basketball friends showed up on the court wearing a wave cap, a thin, nylon hat stretched over his skull. I had never seen one before, so I began to playfully poke a bit of fun. I thought our friendship allowed for it, since we played basketball together frequently. A mutual friend on the court pulled me aside and set me straight. He warned me that I was crossing a cultural line that would cause my friend to be angry. Honestly, I had no idea that my words were hurtful. We talked trash to each other all the time on the court. But there was a line that I had crossed, so I apologized and learned a valuable lesson.

The Dreaded "R" Word

 I still think most of the hurtful things said to me were intended to be hurtful. I find it hard to believe that someone asking why your son doesn't "date your own kind" would be unaware of the racial bias in such an inquiry.

 I happen to agree. In his mind, he was a devout Christian who would never admit to having racist thoughts—despite the inappropriate nature of his question. Most of us have a difficult time admitting our racist tendencies or our racial insensitivity, even when they're pointed out. This is the dreaded "R" word.

I extensively studied the concept of *New Racism,* or aversive racism, in graduate school while at Walden University. Aversive racism is not out loud, aggressive, or even the chanting of racial slurs. It's not people with extreme views. Aversive racism is covert in nature. It's quiet and even friendly. It may believe we can be together in restaurants. We can go to school together. We can live in neighborhoods together and go to work together. We can even go to church together.

Yet when it comes to an issue like marriage, we need to marry people who only look like us. When we purchase a home, it is often among people who look like us. In other words, there are still negative connotations in play that are deep-seated for different races. Those negative thoughts affect our views and behavior toward others.

 One of my friends, who grew up in the south, had a conversation with his daughter before she journeyed off to college. He wanted to warn her of the family complications that could arise if she fell in love with a black man, but he didn't want to admit that was his concern. As many parents do, he talked all around the issue without really saying what he meant. He lectured her about falling in love and marrying someone with whom she had a lot in common. His daughter, however, knew exactly what he was implying. When he finished, she leaned toward him and said, "Don't worry Dad, I'm not going to fall in love with a Republican!"

What an epic response! Her career path eventually took her to South Africa where she ended up marrying a man from Nigeria and her father is delighted.

What a great story! It illustrates the fact that initially your friend felt that some people are not equal to others. Every community has to deal with this since racism dwells in individual hearts and minds. I have a friend of Mexican descent who married a black person. Her dad reacted in the extreme, disowning her for a while, causing her an intense amount of pain. That's what friendly fire does. It heightens pain levels—especially when it's said by someone divinely assigned to us, like a parent.

Most of us want to associate the "R" word with white supremacists and those of their ilk. That allows us to feel as if we're a bit above the fray. Racial conditioning transcends race. Bishop Desmond Tutu, a champion of freedom in South Africa, told the story about being on a flight where he discovered that both the pilot and first officer on that particular journey were black men. He recalled it as one of the proudest moments of his life. During the flight, however, he noted his surprised nervousness wondering if those men had the necessary skills and experience.

The moment we think someone who is racially different is inferior, racism has entered our reality. There is no group at the top or bottom of the totem pole. I once needed to borrow something from a close friend. She told me she was going to be out of town, so she would leave the items on her back porch for me to retrieve. I had to tell her that I wouldn't be able to come and get the items and, of course, she wanted to know why.

"Why can't you come and get something off my back porch?" she asked. I then had to let her into my world a bit. "What will your neighbors think when a black woman goes to the back of your house? They don't know anything about our relationship. They will only know that you are on vacation and a black woman is in your backyard."

She was embarrassed, admitting that she never considered that I might encounter a problem being in her yard. It was a simple lack of knowledge on her part and I told her no apology was necessary.

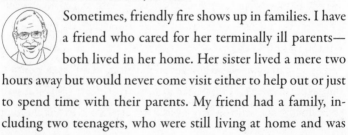 A few years ago, we had friends visit for a weekend. During their visit, the husband went out to retrieve something from his car. While in the driveway, my neighbor Lou—an African-American man who happened to be a bona fide war hero during Vietnam—approached him and asked to speak with me. My friend came back in the house in a bit of a panic. "

Bob, you need to go in the front yard right now. There's a man who needs to speak with you and he doesn't look like he belongs in the neighborhood!"

Curious, I asked him what he meant. He said again that the man simply didn't look like he belonged. It turned out to be my neighbor, Lou, who just needed to know if this was the week to put our blue recyclable cans on the curb. I apologized for the behavior of my houseguest. Lou graciously smiled and stated, "It's okay. I get it." We all get it. I had a genuine war hero living next door to me and someone thought he didn't belong. My heart broke and I'm sure his did, as well.

Sometimes, friendly fire shows up in families. I have a friend who cared for her terminally ill parents— both lived in her home. Her sister lived a mere two hours away but would never come visit either to help out or just to spend time with their parents. My friend had a family, including two teenagers, who were still living at home and was exhausted in caring for them.

One day, mom and daughter were talking about the sister who never visited. "I'm fine with it," the mother insisted. "Your sister has a life." I'm sure her mom was only deflecting her own pain by justifying to herself why the older sister never visited. I doubt she ever realized her implication that the daughter caring for her had no life, but it wasn't missed on that daughter.

Finding Our Way Back

 When we encounter friendly fire, it helps if we are not so quick to take offense ourselves, or if we do, to deal with it internally. If we fire back, we can cause irreparable damage. The goal of those who wish to be healers is to become unoffendable. Someone else's carelessness, or even intentional action, doesn't need to have control over me. If I choose to confront the problem, I'll be far more effective if not fueled by being offended.

Friendly fire has a way of disappearing when it's exposed graciously. Speaking up as a third party when we see it can be helpful. We have the ability to broker the language of healing between others. We may hear words that are spoken from another person's perspective and be able to alert the speaker. We can pull a person aside and quietly say, "Hey, do you know what you just said and are you aware that your words could be hurtful?" I've watched you do that, Arnita.

 Awareness is a large part of the battle. Some people are able to hear things from one person that they cannot hear from another. At the end of it all, we are "Team Humanity." We are allies, being more for one another than against.

Friendly fire is a two-way street that requires a recipient *and*

a contributor. And it's a reality that exists in every culture and station of life. When I have been a recipient, I have learned that asking one or two clarifying questions can often defuse its intensity. This takes assertiveness, resolve, and selectivity. If friendly fire comes from a good friend, one occurrence should never be the end of a relationship. Grace plays a part, especially since so much of friendly fire is without malice or intent. We always need to tread carefully so emotions don't hijack the dialogue.

 Recently, I had lunch with a friend I've known for many years. We had a disagreement a year before, and I was unaware how deeply I had wounded him. In reality, because of my words, he had come to lunch ready to do battle. He was still offended from a conversation that had taken place a year earlier and was convinced that I carried offense toward him, but I had come for a different purpose.

Throughout the years, we had partnered to reach the poor and broken of our city, but the pain of our damaged relationship overwhelmed him. I finally put my head down and said, "My dear friend. If you could rip open my chest and see my heart, you would see that I have nothing but love for you. There is no malice. I apologize for my choice of words a year ago. I should have said things in a different way." He responded with tears. It's what he needed to hear from me! We sat and talked through the entire mess. It was important for me to find my way back to relationship with him. And that started by choosing to speak the language of healing.

 "Find my way back." Those are powerful words. That's what it takes to see healing. We all say wrong things or even right things in a wrong way, whether it be in marriage, church, work, or the larger elements of society. We need to continue to be "Team Humanity," where we make mistakes, whether they be in person or online. It becomes imperative that we give the needed grace to find our way back to relationship with one another. That's how life is supposed to work.

We don't need to walk on eggshells; we simply need to do better. We must rise to a higher level of appreciation with one another, whether we are the contributor or the recipient of friendly fire. We give each other the benefit of the doubt. We find the courage and time to find our way back.

We're told to "stop, drop, and roll" as a fire safety technique; maybe we could "pause, think, and then talk" when relationships start to go sideways.

●

Try This

Crawl: *When you're concerned that something you are about to say could be taken wrongly, be honest about your concern as a way to open the door. "Please let me know if I'm saying something inappropriate here, but..."*

Walk: *Write about an instance where you were the instigator of friendly fire toward someone else. What impact did your actions have?*

Run: *Begin to intentionally monitor the sensitivity of your language when you are with people who are racially, culturally, or religiously different from you.*

15

Custodians of a Common Good

———————————————•———————————————

We have arrived at the last chapter. We hope that we have ignited your desire to speak a language of healing wherever you interact with others that look or think differently than you do. If that's all this book does, we will consider it a success.

However, to change the broader conversation in a world tormented by polarizing rhetoric, we hope to inspire a growing number of people to not only speak a language of healing, but also to become custodians of a common good. Of course, we will all look out for our own good and possibly the good of others we consider "our people." But for our society to function effectively, we need a growing number of people to also care about the common good—what is best for all others in our community.

Often our personal good and the common good are in conflict. That's especially true for those in the majority. Every one of us would want to maximize our freedom and opportunity. That can be done, of course, at the expense of the freedom and opportunity for others. As challenging as it might be, the common good seeks to build a society where freedom and opportunity are equal for all of us.

 When I hear the word *custodian,* I'm reminded of my childhood. In school, custodians walked around with a set of keys on their hip, so they could open doors for people. It may not be as simple today as it was then, but when anyone needed access to a room, all they had to do was find the custodian. So, I see a custodian as one who can give access to people who don't have it.

They also pushed a big cart around with brooms and mops because they knew life was messy. They weren't afraid to get their hands dirty to make sure the facility was clean and safe for others.

 When I think of the word *custodian,* I see the word *custody.* It reminds me of the time a friend and her husband asked if we would take custody of their children in the event something happened to both of them. I can remember the overwhelming weight that hit me: "Oh my goodness, you want me and my husband to raise your children?" It wasn't that they didn't have extended family, but they chose us to care for their children if they weren't able to do so. What a huge responsibility! So, I think of a custodian as someone who takes responsibility and cares for whatever has been placed in their trust.

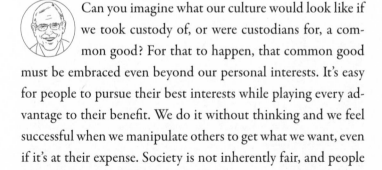 Can you imagine what our culture would look like if we took custody of, or were custodians for, a common good? For that to happen, that common good must be embraced even beyond our personal interests. It's easy for people to pursue their best interests while playing every advantage to their benefit. We do it without thinking and we feel successful when we manipulate others to get what we want, even if it's at their expense. Society is not inherently fair, and people aren't usually conscientious enough to take responsibility for a larger good than their own.

For a generous society to develop and thrive, nothing is more important than shared responsibility where equal opportunity and justice are available to all. That's not just the government's job, it's the responsibility of an engaged citizenry.

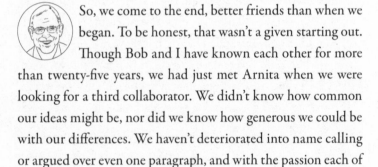

I love that we are just three ordinary people who want common things out of life—love, respect, hope, and justice. It was unlikely we would ever meet! As we have engaged together, we have not argued angrily—even when we didn't see things the same way. We've listened with the goal of writing a book that plows the common ground. No one has tried to upstage the others. We are not academic experts or social scientists conducting elaborate studies. We merely desire to encourage others to embrace a broader and more generous way of looking at those who differ around them.

So, we come to the end, better friends than when we began. To be honest, that wasn't a given starting out. Though Bob and I have known each other for more than twenty-five years, we had just met Arnita when we were looking for a third collaborator. We didn't know how common our ideas might be, nor did we know how generous we could be with our differences. We haven't deteriorated into name calling or argued over even one paragraph, and with the passion each of us carried into this project, I find that incredible.

This was beyond anything I could've imagined when we first met in Dallas. We made a commitment at the beginning that we were going to be collaborative; that was our common good. We knew there were going to be differences of opinion, experience, and preferences, but we were committed to finding the shared space between us. In doing so, not only have our relationships been strengthened, we are all wiser.

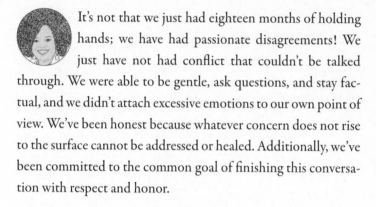

It's not that we just had eighteen months of holding hands; we have had passionate disagreements! We just have not had conflict that couldn't be talked through. We were able to be gentle, ask questions, and stay factual, and we didn't attach excessive emotions to our own point of view. We've been honest because whatever concern does not rise to the surface cannot be addressed or healed. Additionally, we've been committed to the common goal of finishing this conversation with respect and honor.

Rights, Respect, and Responsibility

Our citizenship gives us rights and privileges in our country. Ideally, we all share identical rights and privileges, regardless of agreement or uniformity. Once we shift our mind to embrace commonness—what's good for the goose is good for the gander—we can make progress to overcome the division of our times and get closer to those who differ from us.

Twenty-five years ago, the Freedom Forum First Amendment Center brought together diverse groups of people—politically, socially, religiously—to attempt to define our common good. How do we share public spaces in society while maintaining fairness for those who are different? One of those efforts generated a consensus statement called "Rights, Respect and Responsibility," and another titled "Religion in American Public Life."

Regretfully, most of our progress on civil rights has not come from the majority finding ways to include those who are marginalized by our institutions. It has come by those minority groups having to fight for equal rights in the courts. Not only has progress been slow, but it has also come with animosity and resentment.

One of the brilliant discoveries of this process was to realize that, as Americans, for every right we have there is a corresponding responsibility to protect those rights for others. In negotiating sessions, people had to learn that they best protect their own rights by protecting the rights of those with whom they disagreed. If you want freedom of religion, you also have to defend it for religions other than your own. It's really championing the sanctity of human conscience. Without that, we lose credibility regarding our own rights.

 What a challenge! It takes a certain level of maturity even to say what you just said and to understand reciprocity. Most people are more self-centric than that. Being others-focused requires us to engage our hearts.

 Taking custody of the common good means we must have a different conversation. It's not primarily about policy; it is about the environment in which policies are discussed. Is the common good served by a free college education for all or universal health care? Some would argue, yes. Others will cry socialism in the face of such policies, concerned that increased dependency on the state destroys the personal initiative necessary to build the economic engine that can pay for it all. My personal preference isn't the common good; it's respecting those who see the world differently than I do enough to have a more reasoned conversation than my own self-interest normally allows.

There are always voices left and right that demand society serves their interests alone. That's precisely the way to conflict and eventually civil war. Seeking a common good teaches us to share our culture with fairness and equity. It's the only hope for peace.

What Do You Do with Your Privilege?

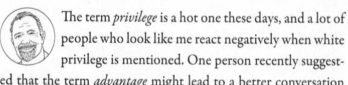 The term *privilege* is a hot one these days, and a lot of people who look like me react negatively when white privilege is mentioned. One person recently suggested that the term *advantage* might lead to a better conversation since it seemed to alleviate the guilt that privilege conveys. He could recognize that he had an advantage, not of his own making, simply because he was born white...

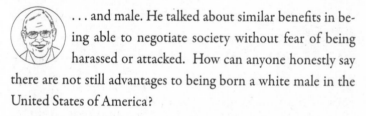 . . . and male. He talked about similar benefits in being able to negotiate society without fear of being harassed or attacked. How can anyone honestly say there are not still advantages to being born a white male in the United States of America?

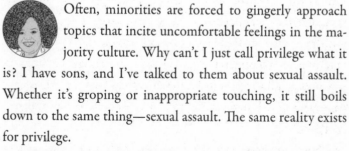 I thought it might be a good idea to get to the same reality without people acknowledging that they had orchestrated their own privilege. But, Arnita, you told me you see that as a cop-out.

Often, minorities are forced to gingerly approach topics that incite uncomfortable feelings in the majority culture. Why can't I just call privilege what it is? I have sons, and I've talked to them about sexual assault. Whether it's groping or inappropriate touching, it still boils down to the same thing—sexual assault. The same reality exists for privilege.

I am a minority and I want you to be comfortable enough to understand you have it, while also further understanding that we know it exists for you. This acknowledgment builds the necessary trust to forge healing relationships. White privilege has nothing to do with money or status, grit or drive. It has everything to do with skin color.

Skin color holds meaning, whether it be good, bad, or indifferent. For some, skin color is a positive. For others, it carries a stigma. Skin color can be an advantage. If we are both in a store and both need assistance, you will likely be offered help before me—just because you're white. It's that simple. It's not malicious or crazy; it's just how it is. Your skin color is not causing you further problems; mine may.

 One of the illustrations that really helped drive that home to me was a conversation about being right- or left-handed. If you're right-handed, you have an advantage in the culture. Most things are designed for you because you're in the majority. I've had an appreciation of my white privilege for a while. It doesn't mean someone like me hasn't had challenges, but one barrier I've never had to face was my skin color.

The more significant issue is that if you have privileges in an inequitable culture, take the responsibility to help expand that access to others. Advantage does not have to be exploited for my benefit alone; I can use it to open opportunities for others who don't have it. Now, we're back to the common good—helping others have the same benefits I enjoy. When I am a custodian of the common good, I can help unlock access to others who have been shut out.

Take Responsibility Where You Are

 It might be a good idea for those with a privilege to resist omitting people outside your culture. I'm convinced that if those who hold power in our country changed just that one thing, the whole currency and culture of the United States would improve.

For much of my life, I've identified as an American with as much passion as I did a Christian. I have learned to see our society and the world as having equal value. It's wonderful to love our home nation and take pride in her accomplishments, but not at the expense of diminishing the rest of the world.

Until we change the way we think in our home towns, nothing will change in Washington. It's important to live in a way that honors others, but it needs to be where we have influence: work, school, community. If we can ignite people to live differently in their own relationships, change will be the inevitable result. If we don't take those steps, we'll be right here in twenty-five years, still battling the venom of a hostile society.

Leaders have to lead, whether they are at home, work, church, or in the community. It's imperative that they be both strategic and intentional to invite diverse voices into the conversation. For some leaders this will be effortless; for others it will require an adjustment in their leadership style. These changes come one act at a time and trickle down to shape others with positive change.

If we desire to take custody of the common good, it helps first to understand our identity. If we only identify as political, that's the only thing we'll see. It becomes difficult to see life through any other filter. If we only identify racially, we'll be hemmed in by that filter, as well. This is a call to diversify our thinking. There are 7.5 billion people on the Earth, and they all have one thing in common—they are human beings made in the image and likeness of their Creator.

 If I only identify as female, I won't see life through any other filter. I choose to identify as human as my most salient identifier. After that, I'm a Christian. Our identifiers are personal and subjective, but they deeply color our experience. Healing is possible when we learn to connect with others based on what we hold in common while respecting each other in our differences.

 Twenty years ago I counseled a pastor who struggled with his sexuality. He was married with children but would also clandestinely meet men. One day, I asked him to pull back the curtain and take me where he went. He began to weep and said, "You would really do this for me?"

I found myself in a public park at 11:30 at night on a Tuesday in January. It was 32 degrees, and the fog was so thick I could barely see. As my eyes adjusted, I could see men everywhere. One was on a bench. Another was next to a tree. On a Tuesday night at 11:30. I'll never forget the loneliness, with the hope that someone would see them and tell them they were okay. It helped me understand my friend's pain and, after that night, he began to trust me with more of his life. It was vital for me to merely say, "I'm interested enough to spend time with you in your world." The intentional nurturing of individual relationships will lead to our passion for the common ground.

 Our voices are also critical to lowering the anxious and divisive rhetoric to a level where we are able to hear one another. Our demeanor is as important as our words. We can choose not to be offended easily, even in the midst of difficult conversations. We can choose to treat others with respect and kindness. And we can tell stories from our lives while inviting others to share stories from theirs.

Since an overbearing presence can squelch the voices of others, there have been times when I've had to confront the bully in the room. "Excuse me? Do you really mean what you are saying?" Or, "Did you hear what she just said?" It's crucial to ask honest, direct questions to create thought and discussion beyond one person's version of the truth. When public policy is discussed, many have a tendency to exceed their knowledge or experience. It's like sports talk radio. It's easy to call on Monday morning about a play and criticize a coach or player because you were never in the competition. You didn't risk anything. Speculation is not engagement; opinion is not fact.

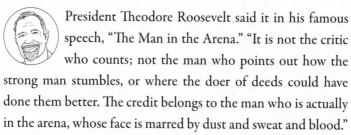 President Theodore Roosevelt said it in his famous speech, "The Man in the Arena." "It is not the critic who counts; not the man who points out how the strong man stumbles, or where the doer of deeds could have done them better. The credit belongs to the man who is actually in the arena, whose face is marred by dust and sweat and blood."

The reality of a twenty-four-hour news cycle has come with a price, as nearly all of us have embraced the role of critic. Our society needs participants above critics.

Helping others find their voice is one of the most significant and fulfilling parts of my existence. Everyone must do their own soul-searching to discover what we want to advocate. When we commit to collaborate, we are able to pool and share ideas and outcomes that have the power to change the way we think.

Embracing a Broader World

 Collaboration can only begin when we start to see the world through someone else's eyes. Initially, don't worry about whether you agree; just process their input based on their experience. Many of our long-held positions may be merely a result of our life experiences or lack of them. That doesn't make it wrong, but it does mean it's not a complete answer either.

The idea of collaboration recognizes that other people possess wisdom I don't have. If I can be open to that wisdom, my world expands. When making group decisions, the intentional act of inviting a broad cross-section of people is a significant step forward. Listen to each other's stories and ideas. You'll see how conclusions different from your own can add wisdom and flavor to your personal approach.

The first half of my life didn't lend itself to collaboration because I was confident of my convictions and thought my views were important for others to hear. Now that I know my view of the universe is skewed by my experience, which includes the privileges I've had, I want to listen to the opinions of others. I want to hear what they are thinking, especially if my first reaction is to disagree. I'm going to let their input sit on my heart for a few days, especially if it's something personal. I'll withhold judgment to give myself time to think about it. I may discuss it with others: "Someone said this is a blind spot of mine. What do you think?"

I have a much different perception of how much reality I see. I used to think I saw a huge slice of it, now I know it is but a narrow slice. I always benefit by bringing someone who has a different slice into the conversation.

Often, those who've never had to see the world from another viewpoint, don't understand the importance. Many can live their whole lives without doing so. Those who want to speak a language of healing, however, will embrace a more growth-minded mentality. Our thinking changes first, then our behavior follows.

 For any positive change to take place, we must first see the need. Once we see, our desires will hopefully lead us to action. As a custodian of the common good, it has become my mission to help people understand. And to help them change.

Will you join us? The language of healing is the verbal tools, temperament, and compassion to draw people out of their fears and divisiveness and invite them to more active engagement with all kinds of people around them.

It may seem a daunting task, but it simply begins with how I treat the next person I'm with, who I'll meet at the next gathering, or how I approach a stranger.

Mother Teresa said it well in *No Greater Love*:

> *Peace and war start within one's own home. If we really want peace for the world, let us start by loving one another within our families. Sometimes it is hard for us to smile at one another. In order for love to be genuine, it has to be above all, a love for our neighbor. We must love those who are nearest to us, in our own family. From there, love spreads toward whoever may need us. It is easy to love those who live far away. It is not always easy to love those who live right next to us.*

●

Try This

Crawl: *According to Harvard Business Review, many times in situations needing innovation and creativity, the phrase, "How might we . . . ?" is crucial. It is inclusive and open language allowing many options to be considered for a win-win situation. Use it often when collaborating with people who differ.*

Walk: *Where can you be a voice for a common good that rises above your own personal preferences?*

Run: *Find one person who is disadvantaged and do something to open access for them in a way they can't do for themselves.*

Acknowledgements

All three of us are incredibly grateful for how the other two engaged this process. No one was asked to compromise their voice or their ideas, and each kept working toward the goal of creating an experience that would help others enjoy the same kind of conversations that we shared together. It was such a risk starting out and this project could have easily gone sideways, but the diligence, generosity, and honesty we had with one another kept us on track.

To work for more than a year and a half together without anger, hurt feelings, or even someone trying to climb to the top of the heap has truly been a joyful and transforming experience for each of us.

We also want to acknowledge the craftsmen and women who have helped bring this dream to fruition:

Kyle and Jess Rice at Blue Sheep Media chose our book to launch their new publishing company in Wyoming. They have been enthusiastic supporters of this message and diligent in the process of bringing it to print, all while negotiating a new pregnancy as well.

Kate Lapin has been Wayne's editor on so many projects, and we were grateful she made time to work on this one with us. She's a master at this. If you find mistakes anywhere, assume that was us still tweaking until the last possible minute. She uses Chicago Manual of Style and is a minimalist with commas, which we enjoy.

Charles Brock of brockbookdesignco.com captured the heart of this book in a very simple but poignant cover. We all went "Wow!" when we first saw it and hope it conveys to others the hope that we can be better than the issues that divide us. Nan Bishop did the typesetting and she's such a delightful stickler for details.

Murry Whitman drew those lovely caricatures that helped you find your way through our conversation. He captured not only or likenesses but some of our personality as well.

And of course, we all have people in our lives, too numerous to mention, who have been our cheerleaders and supporters as we have grown to embrace these realities and as we found one another to write them down to share with a wider world. But here are a few thanks from each of us:

From Arnita

To God for His unwavering love shown to me, once again, by orchestrating my being invited to my men, Michael, Evan, and Nolan for being my life posse, making me smile, and being the best chapters of my life story.

From Bob

To my partner in life, Danette, for loving me through every step as we raised three daughters—Liz, Kendra, and Jessica—and now reap the rewards of the journey with three sons-in-law and ten incredible grandchildren.

To Paul Swearingen, Ken Joy, and Al Jones for every encouragement along the way. To Emad Meerza, my dear friend and partner in media, who has opened my eyes a bit wider to those who see the world through a different lens. Without him, I'm not sure this book would exist. And of course, to the Lord Himself, who found me when I was simply unable to find Him.

From Wayne

I have so many friends from around the world who have helped shape my life and influenced my journey in learning a language of healing. They are too numerous to name, but I am grateful for every friendship I have and the wisdom I've gained.

The First Amendment Freedom Forum and Dr. Charles Haynes were a great help in my work with BridgeBuilders to understand the law and our founding documents as it relates to this topic. Properly applied, they provide a rich framework to teach us how to respect our differences and stake out a common ground that enriches us all.

And of course, my family provides the glorious environment of love and joy out of which I get to write and travel. My wife, Sara, of forty-four years, and my two adult children and their families make my life full and rich.

About the Authors

Wayne Jacobsen

Wayne travels the world as an author and speaker on themes of spiritual intimacy and relational community, especially where people are in crisis. Some of his popular books include *He Loves Me*, *Finding Church*, and *A Man Like No Other*. He was also a coauthor and publisher of *The Shack*. The words *self-effacing* and *best-selling author* aren't often used together, but Wayne's insight and humor have opened doors around the world whether it means resolving religious–liberty conflicts in public education, helping starving tribes in Kenya build a viable economy, or helping people find a vibrant spiritual life.

A former pastor, Wayne now hosts Lifestream.org, which provides resources for spiritual growth, and a podcast at TheGodJourney.com to encourage people thinking outside the box of organized religion. Both have inspired countless people to a more vibrant faith and a greater understanding of living in the church Jesus is building in the world. He lives in Southern California with Sara, his wife of forty-four years, where they both enjoy their adult children and grandchildren.

Arnita Willis Taylor

Wise, practical, resourceful, and fun, Arnita relates to diverse people and helps them maximize their potential. She has an inspiring way of equipping people as a leader, minister, mentor, and coach. She is known for her gregarious personality and warm hospitality to guests in her home.

From Murfreesboro, Tennessee, Arnita graduated from the University of Tennessee-Knoxville with a degree in Medical Technology and earned her master's degree in Leadership from Walden University. Her professional background runs from clinical laboratory science to small groups pastoral ministry. As the founder of

EIGHT Leadership Development Group, Arnita serves leaders by assisting individuals, teams, and organizations. She is a passionate communicator who helps enrich and empower others, and because she intentionally places herself in diversified settings she regularly teaches across racial, denominational, and gender lines.

At home in Keller, Texas, she is the wife of thirty-one years to Michael and the proud and grateful mother of two sons, Evan and Nolan.

Robert L. "Bob" Prater

Bob Prater is a lover of God and also a lover of—and advocate for—people. With a background in business, media, and ministry, he is half of the podcast *A Christian & A Muslim Walk into a Studio* alongside American-Muslim leader, Emad Meerza. He spent several years in full-time ministry as both a pastor and an administrator.

He has started businesses as diverse as developing and producing for television to selling whatever he can find online, and he has been in the top 3 percent of online sellers in the world. Bob married his high school sweetheart, Danette, in Eugene, Oregon, more than forty years go. As the dad to three daughters and three sons-in-law, and the grandpa to ten grandchildren, he leads a small army as Santa each year to the forgotten and abandoned places where the poorest reside. He also functions as an "Elder at Large," helping people connect dots in his hometown of Bakersfield, California.

Pass It On!

A Language of Healing for a Polarized Nation doesn't have a gigantic publishing machine behind it. We hope to inspire a grassroots effort of people who fundamentally want to change the conversation in this country.

If you're passionate about the content here, we would appreciate you helping us get the word out. We want you to open the doors of conversations to people you don't consider part of your tribe, not to convince them of your opinions, but to listen to theirs in the light of their own story. We want to invite you to work with others not fighting over binary options but looking for the broader common ground that makes room for a wide diversity of views.

And if you would be so kind, we would like you to pass that message along to others. Here are some ways you can do that:

- Find some of the *Crawl, Walk, and Run* exercises at the end of each chapter that you can use to change the way you live and engage people around you.

- Buy some extra copies of this book to pass out to others who might benefit from its message. As one archconservative told us, "This book gave me ideas that I'd never considered before." If you want to buy them by the case, we can find special case pricing at bluesheepmedia.com.

- Form a book group with some people you know—or even acquaintances—and explore it together.

- Quote liberally from the book in your social media. Create memes from some of the endorsements at the front of the book or quotations from the book that encourage or enlighten you, such as the following:

  - This book is for those who want to find ways to communicate and cooperate beyond our most deeply rooted differences, realizing that in the shared spaces of our society we have more to gain through mutual understanding than the politics of polarization.

- Do we want to live in a society where divergent tribes fight over who can gain the most advantage for themselves through legislation and public perception, or do we want to build a society that is fair for all, despite our differences?

- When you get close to people, you'll find they are just like you. That's where compassion can take root.

- When you combine courage with compassion, the world can change.

- There are always voices left and right that demand society serves their interests alone. That's precisely the way to conflict and eventually civil war. Seeking a common good teaches us to share our culture with fairness and equity. It's the only hope for peace.

- Our identifiers are personal and subjective, but they deeply color our experience. Healing is possible when we learn to connect with others based on what we hold in common while respecting each other in our differences.

- The greatest challenge in building an equitable society is to find a way to share power with those groups who have been traditionally left out. For that to happen, those who already have a seat at the table have to make a path for those who are not.

- Many of our long-held positions may merely be a result of our life experiences or lack of them. That doesn't make it wrong, but it does mean it's not a complete answer either.

- The vast majority of people are reasonable enough to have the conversation we're suggesting. The problem is the microphones are in the hands of those who are on the extremes: those who have something to gain from exacerbating the conflict, rather than resolving it.

- We're inviting people away from the fringes of imagined superiority, back to the middle where shared values cross diverse lines.

- The most powerful voice at the table is not the person speaking up for their own vested interest, but the one who defends the rights of opposition when they are being crowded out of the conversation.